ANNUAL UPDATE

UK POLITICS

Nick Gallop
Maria Egan

HODDER
EDUCATION
AN HACHETTE UK COMPANY

Although every effort has been made to ensure that website addresses are correct at time of going to press, Hodder Education cannot be held responsible for the content of any website mentioned in this book. It is sometimes possible to find a relocated web page by typing in the address of the home page for a website in the URL window of your browser.

Hachette UK's policy is to use papers that are natural, renewable and recyclable products and made from wood grown in well-managed forests and other controlled sources. The logging and manufacturing processes are expected to conform to the environmental regulations of the country of origin.

Orders: please contact Hachette UK Distribution, Hely Hutchinson Centre, Milton Road, Didcot, Oxfordshire, OX11 7HH. Telephone: +44 (0)1235 827827. Email education@hachette.co.uk. Lines are open from 9 a.m. to 5 p.m., Monday to Friday. You can also order through our website: www.hoddereducation.co.uk

ISBN: 978 1 3983 8457 6
© Nick Gallop and Maria Egan 2023
First published in 2023 by
Hodder Education,
An Hachette UK Company
Carmelite House
50 Victoria Embankment
London EC4Y 0DZ
www.hoddereducation.co.uk
Impression number   5 4 3 2 1
Year   2027 2026 2025 2024 2023

Cover photo © Rawpixel Ltd – stock.adobe.com
Illustrations by Aptara, Inc.
Typeset in India by Aptara, Inc.
Printed in the UK by CPI Print

A catalogue record for this title is available from the British Library.

Contents

Contents

Chapter 1

Think tanks: how do they operate and why are they controversial?

Focus

Examination specifications place think tanks under the broader heading of pressure groups, and require an understanding of the methods they use to exert power. Students need to be able to evaluate the extent to which think tanks can influence both the government and members of parliament.

Edexcel	UK Politics 1.3	Pressure groups and other influences
AQA	3.1.2.4	Pressure groups

Context

Think tanks are organisations that suggest approaches to particular political, social or economic issues. They aim to shape and influence public discussion of politics as well as to guide the actions of governments. Although often established by those who wish to promote specific political viewpoints, they can be sources of considerable expertise. Their research papers and policy ideas can make them a valuable political resource.

Think tanks are well established within the British political system. The Centre for Policy Studies, which was founded in 1974, helped set the stage for the election of Margaret Thatcher in 1979. The Institute for Public Policy Research played a similar role for Tony Blair in the 1990s. The existence of think tanks may be nothing new but their numbers and the extent of their political involvement have both grown considerably in recent years. Their increasing strength and presence makes an assessment of their current role timely.

How do think tanks operate?

Think tanks vary in size, ambition and ways of operating but some generalisations can be made about their activities:

- Think tanks publish studies on issues that interest them. These can be justifications for particular policies or explanations of how a think tank believes the business of government should be conducted. For example, in June 2022 the Institute for Government issued 'How metro mayors can help level up England'. In the same month, the Adam Smith Institute released a paper entitled 'Countdown: reforming the Cabinet Office', which explored how to make the Cabinet Office more efficient and effective. It released this paper because it is opposed to bureaucracy and believes that government should be small. Among the suggestions made in the paper was reducing the size of the Cabinet Office by 90%; outsourcing some work currently done by the Cabinet Office to private bodies; and keeping a tighter grip on spending within the Cabinet Office. Sometimes think tanks present original social or economic research and suggest the best responses to the information provided. The Joseph Rowntree Foundation's 2022 UK Poverty Report was a wide-reaching examination of the causes of poverty and its impacts, including its effects on children, the disabled and those from different ethnic groups.

- A few think tanks also publish books. The international affairs think tank, Chatham House, is behind the 'Insights' series. These books are intended to provide readers with a better understanding of key international issues confronting policy makers today. For example, 2022 saw the publication of *The Justice Laboratory: International Law in Africa* by Kerstin Bree Carlson.
- Think tanks act as pressure groups, seeking to influence politicians at all levels. Holding meetings with backbench MPs and government ministers enables them to promote their agendas and suggest courses of action.
- Think tanks aim to forge close links with media outlets, so that their perspectives and research gain publicity.
- Think tanks work to establish themselves as experts in their field, so that the information they provide is respected. Working with academics can help achieve this, as can the recognition gained by being asked to give evidence before select or public bill committees.

How influential are think tanks?

The short answer to this question is 'more than ever'. Examples and specific information will help to illustrate the extent of their power in Britain today.

Think tanks provide information that government departments draw on when drafting legislation. The three think tanks most often cited in policy documents between 2015 and 2021 were:

- The Joseph Rowntree Foundation, which was name-checked in 157 documents, most relating to employment, culture or education. The Joseph Rowntree Foundation is a charity that researches social policy and campaigns on quality of life issues.
- The Institute for Fiscal Studies, a research institute with particular interest in taxation, welfare benefits and education, which received citations in 150 documents.
- The National Bureau of Economic Research, a non-profit American group, which was mentioned in 130 policy documents.

Think tanks can also directly influence government policy. Under Johnson, the Institute for Economic Affairs and the Legatum Institute did much to guide Brexit policy, including the decision to withdraw from the customs union and the single market when leaving the EU. The Policy Exchange document 'Rethinking the planning system for the 21st century' was clearly the primary influence on the Johnson government's proposals to reform planning laws. That these reforms might not be enacted because of their unpopularity with Conservative voters is a reminder that neither think tanks nor governments can necessarily achieve their aims.

Think tanks do not simply shape specific policies. They help formulate the wider priorities of political parties. The 2019 Conservative election manifesto was co-authored by Robert Colville and Rachel Wolf, both of the Centre for Policy Studies, and Munira Mirza, then working at Number 10's Policy Unit. The Labour manifesto for the same election owed a debt to both the Institute for Public Policy Research and the New Economics Foundation in its sections on economic and environmental policy. The think tank Autonomy was behind its proposals for a 4-day working week. The fact that some political catchphrases originate from think tanks is also a testament to their success in embedding their perspectives within political debate. It is from Onward that we get the phrases 'red wall' and 'Workington man', while the expression 'levelling up' is thought to come from the Centre for Policy Studies.

The question will always arise of how far think tanks influence policy or how far they have influence simply because their views and those of the government happen to align. Governments are, of course, subject to many pressures and no government is so easily influenced that it would adopt a policy merely because a think tank were enthusiastic about it. There is evidence, however, that, over time, think tanks can normalise ideas that at first seem outlandish and thus set the groundwork for the later acceptance of these policies. For example, the Adam Smith Institute has been arguing since the 1980s that the British government has a responsibility towards Hong Kong nationals. The case made by the Adam Smith Institute for granting British citizenship to residents of Hong Kong has helped foster acceptance for this policy among Conservative MPs and within the media. This eased its introduction in 2021.

Many politicians work for think tanks before entering parliament, and retain close links with their former employers. In 2022, the Institute of Economic Affairs could boast that four of its former employees were at the top of the Johnson government: Priti Patel, Liz Truss, Dominic Raab and Kwasi Kwarteng. During her time in office, Truss held a number of meetings with the Institute for Economic Affairs. Since these meetings are officially considered to be 'private discussions' there is no record of what Truss and representatives from the Institute of Economic Affairs discussed. This makes it impossible to judge how the latter might have shaped the former's thinking. Many of those who advise government ministers also come from think tanks. Andrew Griffith was chair of the advisory board at the Centre for Policy Studies before becoming head of Number 10's Policy Unit under Johnson in 2022. Both Andrew Gilligan, who advised Johnson on transport, and John Bew, a foreign policy expert employed by the Policy Unit, also spent time at Policy Exchange.

Think tanks have clout within the media partly because some of those who work for them are also employed as political commentators. Robert Colville, for example, is director of the Centre for Policy Studies, and also writes regularly for the *Times*. Daniel Finkelstein, who chairs the chief advisory board at Onward, is also a *Times* columnist. The links between think tanks and journalism can be less obvious but still detectable. Ed Miliband's columns in the *Observer* have often promoted the work of the Resolution Foundation. The chief executive of that think tank, Torsten Bell, used to be a political advisor to Miliband and the two men remain close.

Case study 1.1: The King's Fund 2022

The King's Fund is an independent health think tank that works with the government, health care professionals, charitable and voluntary organisations and local communities on issues related to health, social care and wellbeing. One of the key projects for the King's Fund in 2022 concerned the Health and Care Act, passed that same year. The King's Fund advised the government on aspects of the legislation, which fulfilled one of the think tank's long-term objectives by better integrating health and social care. After the Health and Care Act was passed through parliament, the King's Fund devoted resources to explaining and analysing aspects of the law. For example, its May 2022 paper 'The Health and Care Act: six key questions' examines how the act has changed health care provision and the practical impacts of this.

The ten most influential think tanks in the UK, as ranked by *Mace* Magazine, are shown in Table 1.1. *Mace Magazine* describes itself as 'a cross party political magazine… that aims to become the definitive insider guide to British political power, influence and access'.

Table 1.1 The ten most influential think tanks in the UK

	Think tank	Political orientation	Key aims
1	Centre for Policy Studies	right of centre	to champion the free market and the small state
2	Policy Exchange	right of centre	to formulate policies aimed at improving the delivery of public services, strengthening society and creating a stronger economy
3	Institute for Fiscal Studies	independent	to consider the impact of economic and social policies on society
4	Resolution Foundation	left of centre	to support those on low and middle incomes
5	Institute for Government	independent	to improve the working practices within government

	Think tank	Political orientation	Key aims
6	Institute for Public Policy Research	left leaning	to provide education on a wide range of economic, political and social issues, and to alleviate poverty
7	Institute of Economic Affairs	libertarian	to explain how free economic markets can solve problems facing society
8	Adam Smith Institute	libertarian	to improve understanding of neo-liberal political responses
9	New Economic Foundation	left leaning	to champion social, economic and environmental policies that promote just outcomes
10	Onward	right of centre	to improve the economic chances of those living throughout the UK

Source: https://macemagazine.com/wonk-warriors/

Why are think tanks controversial?

Much of the work done by think tanks takes place in private. There will always be unease about unelected bodies that wield power in ways that are not completely visible, but this sense of unease has increased the longer the Conservative Party has been in power. Johnson's Conservatives were accused not simply of working with think tanks but of allowing them a level of access to government business unprecedented in previous administrations. Johnson's actions as secretary of state for foreign affairs perhaps provided a clue to his willingness to do favours for think tanks. In February 2018 Johnson allowed the think tank Initiative for Free Trade to use the Map Room at the Foreign Office for free for their launch event. Sue Grey, the head of ethics at the Cabinet Office, criticised Johnson's decision, saying that the think tank should have paid the normal commercial rate for the use of the room.

Case study 1.2: The Atlas Network

Think tanks in the Atlas Network have formed especially close ties with the Conservative government. British and US think tanks collaborate within the Atlas Network, which comprises more than 450 think tanks worldwide. The Atlas Network is controversial for its working methods. Each of the think tanks within the Atlas Network is an independent organisation but they also co-operate with their partners in the network to advance their aims. These working relationships provide the individual think tanks within the Atlas Network with a level of influence and leverage they would almost certainly not have on their own.

For example, the Institute for Economic Affairs, the Legatum Institute and the Initiative for Free Trade worked with US think tanks the American Enterprise Institute and the Heritage Foundation to produce policy documents on Brexit. The subsequent direction of Brexit policy, combined with the fact that Boris Johnson and Michael Gove visited the US for meetings with the American Enterprise Institute and the Heritage Foundation, contributed to a feeling that British policy was being forged elsewhere. The methods used within the Atlas Network are legitimate operational tactics, of which the Atlas Network makes no secret. It has primarily attracted criticism from those on the left politically, who object to the right-wing agenda pursued by the Atlas Network. That there is no similar left-wing grouping of think tanks to balance out the influence of the right-wing organisations probably drives some of this criticism.

Another controversy surrounding members of the Atlas Network involves their sources of funding. In the last decade, the TaxPayers' Alliance, the Institute of Economic Affairs, Policy Exchange, the Adam Smith Institute and the Legatum Institute have accepted $9 million in contributions from US donors. Two-thirds of this money has found its way to the UK. This means that proceeds from foreign donors are being spent on influencing the British public and its politicians. Loopholes in legislation mean that this is not illegal, but some see it as undermining democracy. What is unusual is not that this issue over funding has arisen but that it is known about. Many think tanks are not transparent about how they are funded. This tends to be more of a problem with think tanks on the right, than those on the left, with the latter more inclined to publicly list their donors. Think tanks that do not name those who fund them justify their decision to preserve their donors' anonymity on the grounds of privacy. Among those think tanks that do not routinely name those from whom they receive funds are the Centre for Policy Studies and the Adam Smith Institute. The Atlas Group of think tanks accepts donations from the oil industry, tobacco companies, wealthy financiers and hedge fund managers. These are not groups that can be said to be representative of wider society.

Furthermore, there is a suspicion that these donations sway the priorities of think tanks. For example, ExxonMobile donated $30,000 to Policy Exchange in 2017. Policy Exchange then began to advocate for legislation that would make it easier to crack down on environmental protestors of the kind that have proved a particular nuisance to ExxonMobile. Policy Exchange and ExxonMobile had their reward in 2022 with passing of the Police, Crime, Sentencing and Courts Act, which made even peaceful protests more difficult to organise.

Think tanks have proliferated in number in recent years. The greater number of groups trying to gain the ear of politicians means more pressure is being exerted on our elected officials. This matters, especially when politicians seem too close to particular think tanks. Priti Patel sat on the advisory council at the Henry Jackson Foundation from 2013–16. She has also accepted funding from the Henry Jackson Foundation and hosted an event for them in parliament. The Henry Jackson Foundation has close connections with America's Central Intelligence Agency, which has long sought the extradition to the US of

Wikileaks founder Julian Assange. When Patel agreed that Assange should be extradited in 2022, the Consortium News website reported their suspicion that the Henry Jackson Foundation had influenced her thinking on that issue.

All think tanks strive to have a strong media profile. Since journalists tend to accord those who represent think tanks a high level of status and respect, as experts in a given field, this can provide think tanks with a level of power that is not merited by the popularity or representative nature of their ideas. A related problem can occur if several small think tanks campaign for the same policy outcome. This can give the false impression that a policy has greater credibility than it deserves. The same phenomenon of many small groups backing a particular policy can make that policy seem more popular than it actually is, which might sway both politicians and voters. All this explains why the Adam Smith Institute, the Institute for Economic Affairs and the TaxPayers' Alliance held regular meetings to agree a common line on Brexit. They thought having a united front on this issue would give them more power to influence policy.

Many think tanks are also registered charities and, as such, benefit from considerable tax breaks. The charitable status of organisations such as the Henry Jackson Society, the Institute for Public Policy Research, the New Economics Foundation, Policy Exchange and the Institute for Economic Affairs rests on their educational work — the efforts they make to inform the public about particular social, economic and political problems. Think tanks that are charities should not present any information which is biased or one sided or that advocates for particular policy outcomes. The Charity Commission has shown concern that not all the think tanks that fall under their remit are sufficiently rigorous in maintaining political neutrality, and in a 2018 regulatory alert issued specific guidance to think tanks on their responsibility for 'avoiding unacceptable political activity'.

How do think tanks assess their role in 2022?

Smart Thinking is a network of UK think tanks. It has a broad range of members from across the political spectrum, and works with them all to publicise their policy ideas and research findings. In 2022, Smart Thinking surveyed 50 of their think tanks to try to better understand the nature of their work and what they thought to be the main difficulties facing them for the future. The results of the survey provide a useful insight into how think tanks assess their role in the political system.

A majority of think tanks (64%) say their key aim is to influence politicians and it is on persuading that group to adopt their ideas that they focus their efforts. Only 1% of groups put targeting the general public as their number one priority, although 83% of groups agreed that educating the public was an important goal for them. Of the remaining groups, 17% said that they prioritised reaching out to the civil service, 14% to the media and 3% to business groups.

The top five policy areas for think tanks are listed in the Smart Thinking report as 'economics, government, international development, international relations and the environment'. In 2020 that list read 'international relations, economics, international development, health, society and diversity'. The two specific policies think tanks saw as the most important going forward were work to achieve net zero and responding to the cost of living crisis. The policies prioritised are evidence that think tanks react to events when setting their goals. In terms of the type of work that they prize, 42% of think tanks view research papers as their most useful political output, 37% value their policy recommendations most highly and 13% rate critiquing current policy as their most notable achievement.

Think tanks identified a number of difficulties they needed to address for the future. Of these the top six were:

1 uncertainty about the future direction of politics

2 the poor standard of public discussion

3 an insufficiently diverse workforce within the think tank sector

4 shortage of the money required to fund think tanks

5 the ongoing problems caused by the Covid-19 pandemic

6 lack of public trust in think tanks.

Despite this list, 66% of groups surveyed agreed that they felt positive about the future prospects for think tanks, with 55% of think tanks expecting to increase their numbers of full-time staff within the next 12 months.

Exam success

Think tanks are playing an increasing role in UK political life. They are an informal part of the political process and this means that the influence they exert is sometimes seen as problematic. This is despite the expertise they often inject into political debates and the data they provide to aid political decision making. Questions in this area may be framed as follows:

- *Evaluate the view that the influence that think tanks have over political parties and in parliament undermines democracy in the UK.* (Edexcel style, 30 marks)
- *'Think tanks' influence over political parties and in parliament undermines democracy in the UK.' Analyse and evaluate this statement.* (AQA style, 25 marks)

The best responses will draw on a range of examples of think tank activity. Students should aim to weigh up the democratic benefits think tanks provide, as well as to examine ways in which they could be argued to undermine democracy. Essays should consider the following:

- Think tanks are unelected and unaccountable. Despite this they have enormous power within the political system. For example, the 2019 election manifestos of both major political parties were produced in conjunction with think tanks. The Centre for Policy Studies co-authored the Conservative manifesto. Both the Institute for Public Policy Research and the New Economics Foundation contributed to the Labour manifesto.

It should be noted, though, that think tanks are only awarded this power because their views are in line with those political parties who work with them.

- The work of think tanks is rarely transparent. They are able to hold private discussions with government ministers and MPs of which no record has to be provided. Liz Truss's meetings with the Institute for Economic Affairs during her time as prime minister fall into this category.
- Think tanks employ academics and experts to research and write policy papers. These provide MPs and governments with high-quality evidence on which to base their decision making and voting choices. Think tanks also provide expert advice through seminars and one-to-one meetings.
- Think tanks in the UK represent a whole range of political viewpoints. This enhances democracy by increasing the number of ideas that are discussed and considered.

What next?

Read:

- 'How the right's radical thinktanks reshaped the Conservative Party', 29 November, 2019, *Guardian* (www.theguardian.com).
- 'Wonk Warriors: the think tanks that run the show', *Mace Magazine* (https://macemagazine.com).
- Regulatory alerts, Charity Commission (www.gov.uk).

Research: the work of a prominent think tank, such as the Adam Smith Institute or the Institute for Public Policy Research.

Chapter 2

Rights in context: do we need a British Bill of Rights?

Focus

Examination specifications require students to understand what human rights are and how they have developed over time. Students need to be able to evaluate the impact of parliamentary legislation on the rights that UK citizens can claim and to engage in arguments about the extent to which human rights are protected.

Edexcel	UK Politics 1.4	Rights in context — major milestones in their development and debates on the extent, limits and tensions within the UK's rights-based culture
AQA	3.1.1.1	Contemporary legislation and current issues regarding rights Debates about the extent of rights in the UK

Context

The Human Rights Act, which was passed in 1998, incorporated the European Convention on Human Rights into British law. Before the passing of the act, anyone who felt that their convention rights had been breached had to take their case to the European Court of Human Rights in Strasbourg. This was an expensive undertaking. It also involved a lengthy wait for judicial rulings because the European Court of Human Rights always had a backlog of cases.

Once the Human Rights Act came into force in October 2000 groups and individuals could take their grievances to the British courts. The Human Rights Act, which was passed under Tony Blair's Labour government, has long attracted criticism from the Conservatives. (These criticisms will be discussed later in the chapter.) The 2010 Conservative manifesto promised to repeal the Human Rights Act and pass a British Bill of Rights instead but only since the 2019 election has this policy had genuine momentum behind it. In December 2021, the Johnson government opened a formal consultation on its paper 'Human Rights Act Reform: A Modern Bill of Rights'. The publication of the consultation document restarted the debate about the merits or otherwise of the Human Rights Act. Closely linked to this debate are the arguments about how far the desire to replace the Human Rights Act with a new British Bill of Rights is justified. The consultation closed in April 2022 and Dominic Raab made an official response to the comments the government had received on its proposals. Raab's statement confirmed the government's intention to introduce a bill in line with the government's original intentions. That bill started its passage through the Houses of Parliament in June 2022 but was withdrawn by the Truss government in September. Truss felt that the legislation had not been properly thought through and needed to be substantially reworked. Raab's reappointment as secretary of state for justice by Rishi Sunak signals that the British Bill of Rights is likely to be re-introduced to parliament in the near future.

Box 2.1 What is the European Convention on Human Rights?

The European Convention on Human Rights has nothing to do with the European Union. It is an international treaty, which was drawn up soon after the Second World War. British lawyers were instrumental in the production of the Convention and, in 1951, Britain became the first country to ratify (give official consent to) the Convention, although it did not formally become part of British law until 1953. Today, 46 countries are signed up to the Convention.

The aim of the Convention was to prevent a repeat of the horrors of the Second World War, which had included the genocide of over 6 million Jewish people and half a million Roma. Polish political prisoners, gay people and people with disabilities were also murdered in Nazi concentration camps. The Convention states that human rights are universal. This means that they can be claimed by anyone, anywhere in the world. Among the rights granted by the convention are the right to life, liberty and a fair trial. The Convention also states that individuals should be free from slavery, not subject to torture and allowed freedom of thought, conscience, religion, expression and assembly (to meet freely with people of their choosing).

Under the terms of the Convention, governments have an obligation to protect individuals from human rights abuses. People who feel that their government is failing in this duty can bring a case to the European Court of Human Rights. Judgements made by the European Court are binding on member states, which means that they should change their laws and practices if a judgement goes against them.

Why do the Conservatives want to replace the Human Rights Act with a British Bill of Rights?

There is strong support in the Conservative Party for repealing the Human Rights Act. There are two main reasons why:

1 They want to reduce the number of human rights cases coming before the British courts. The government view is that the provisions of the Human Rights Act allow some 'trivial' cases to come to court. Preventing this will free up court time to focus on more important matters.

2 They want to reassert the sovereignty of parliament in the area of human rights law. At the moment, key decisions on human rights are being made by judges when they interpret the Human Rights Act. The Conservatives stress that lawmakers, not unelected judges, should have the final say on what human rights people can claim. The British Bill of Rights would support this aim by introducing more detailed and specific guidance on the rights to which people are entitled. This would make it clearer what politicians want and reduce the need for judges to decide how laws should be applied.

What changes were proposed by the British Bill of Rights?

The European Convention on Human Rights

Under the terms of the bill, Britain would have remained part of the European Convention on Human Rights. Indeed, the bill reaffirmed Britain's commitment to the European Convention specifically and, more generally, to providing global leadership on human rights issues. Remaining part of the European Convention is important symbolically, and as long as the UK maintains its membership, cases from Britain can continue to be heard in the European Court of Human Rights.

The Convention does not command universal support in the Conservative Party, with the European Research Group of MPs being especially sceptical about it. If another British Bill of Rights were to be drafted, there would be pressure from some in the Conservative parliamentary party to take the radical step of withdrawing from it altogether. This is a move that would be resisted by Labour, the Liberal Democrats and the SNP.

The decision to remain part of the European Convention on Human Rights sat alongside a promise that the Bill of Rights would continue to protect the 'substantive rights' people can currently claim under the Convention. The Bill of Rights also proposed introducing a new right to trial by jury. At the same time, the Bill of Rights would have made it harder for people to bring human rights cases to court. Individuals who felt that their human rights had been infringed would have been required to prove that existing circumstances would have caused them 'significant disadvantage'. Only if they could prove this would they have been granted leave to pursue their case. It was hoped that the introduction into law of this so-called 'permission stage' would result in a decrease in the number of human rights cases.

Box 2.2	Key definition

Substantive rights: basic human rights, such as the rights to life, liberty and property.

The Supreme Court

The Bill of Rights would have enhanced the powers of the Supreme Court in one area of its operations. It would have removed the requirement currently placed on Supreme Court judges to consider precedents from the European Court of Human Rights when making rulings. British judges would not be told to ignore case law from the Strasbourg court. Rather, they would be encouraged to give more weight to UK common law when making their rulings. The government's hope was that this would lead to judicial decisions better tailored to the particular circumstances of the UK.

Right to private and family life

The change described above would have given UK judges more freedom of manoeuvre but it sat alongside changes likely to have the opposite effect. The British Bill of Rights provided more guidance for judges on how to interpret and apply those aspects of human rights law that relate to private and family life. This is a focus for the Conservatives because they believe the Human Rights Act has sometimes been misused to provide protection to people who have shown no respect for the law themselves.

Case study 2.1: AA v Secretary of State for the Home Department

In the July 2022 case AA v Secretary of State for the Home Department, the Supreme Court was asked to consider if Nigerian citizen and convicted drug dealer AA could be deported to Nigeria by the UK government. AA is in a relationship with a British citizen and has a daughter from a previous relationship who is also a UK national. The clauses of the Human Rights Act which protect people's rights to a private and family life allowed the Supreme Court to rule that deporting AA would be 'unduly harsh' on both his current partner and his daughter and that he should be allowed to remain in the UK. The British government's view was that, even if they had ties to the UK, non-British nationals with criminal convictions should not have the right to continue living here. The only specified exception to this made in the Bill of Rights was for individuals at risk of torture in their home countries.

There was another reason why the government wanted to rein in the power of judges to decide when and how far people are entitled to a private life. It felt that the balance between one person's right to privacy and another's right to free expression had tipped too far in favour of the former.

Case study 2.2: ZXC v Bloomberg

The case of ZXC v Bloomberg came before the Supreme Court in February 2022. The verdict reached in the case was that media outlet Bloomberg had been wrong to publish personal details about an American businessman (ZXC) who was under suspicion of criminal activity. The judges ruled that

Bloomberg had breached ZXC's privacy and ordered it to pay him damages of £25,000. A number of journalists expressed unhappiness about the outcome of the case, which they felt undermined their right to report freely on matters of public interest. *The Economist* went so far as to say that the verdict could have 'a chilling effect on high quality journalism'.

Freedom of expression

The Johnson government indicated that it was listening to the concerns of journalists and promised to strengthen the protection around freedom of expression in a second way. It aimed to make it more difficult for the courts to order journalists to disclose the names of people who had provided information for their stories. This proposed change to the law rested on the assumption that better protecting people's right to anonymity would make them feel more able to speak out.

Other changes in the Bill of Rights

The power of judges to impose 'positive obligations' would also have been limited under the Bill of Rights. A positive obligation is a ruling that creates a requirement for a public body to take a particular course of action. An example of a positive obligation being imposed by the Supreme Court is provided by the ruling in the case of MS (Pakistan) v Secretary of State for the Home Department (2020). In their judgement on this case, the justices ruled that the state has a duty to identify and protect victims of human trafficking. A government press release of June 2022 objected to a different positive obligation — one that requires police forces to tell members of gangs about threats made against them by those in other gangs.

Another clause in the bill that would have reduced the power of judges concerned secondary legislation. This is law made by government ministers under powers given to them in acts of parliament, rather than being directly made by parliament. For example, under the terms of the Misuse of Drugs Act 1971, ministers can ban new drugs that they consider harmful without consulting with parliament. Currently, judges can strike down secondary legislation. The British Bill of Rights would have changed this and given judges the power only to declare secondary legislation incompatible with human rights law. Declarations of incompatibility do not force the government to take action; they merely highlight an inconsistency in the law. The government can choose how to respond to them and even to ignore them altogether.

Finally, the British Bill of Rights would have introduced new rules relating to the financial payouts that could be made to those who have suffered human rights abuses. The amount of money to which a person would be entitled would vary according to their past behaviour, with, for example, individuals with criminal convictions given smaller compensation payments than model citizens.

The arguments for and against introducing the British Bill of Rights

The arguments for and against introducing the British Bill of Rights are outlined in Table 2.1.

Table 2.1 The arguments for and against the British Bill of Rights

Arguments for the British Bill of Rights	Arguments against the British Bill of Rights
In returning power over human rights issues to politicians, a British Bill of Rights would reinforce parliamentary sovereignty, which is a key pillar of the UK constitution. It is right and proper that issues as important as what rights British citizens can claim and how and when they can claim them are made by elected, accountable politicians.	The Conservatives emphasise the benefits of the British Bill of Rights for parliamentary sovereignty but opponents have accused them of being more interested in ensuring that judges have a reduced ability to check executive power. Making it more difficult for judges to impose positive obligations and removing the right of judges to strike down secondary legislation could reduce their power over the executive. This is a concern because part of the role of an independent judiciary is to scrutinise the government. Our democracy is only healthy if there are checks and balances in place to prevent the government abusing its power.
The European Convention on Human Rights is over 70 years old and ideas about human rights have changed a lot during that time. For example, the Convention provides no explicit protection for the LGBTQ+ community. It also allows for the imprisonment of 'alcoholics, drug addicts or vagrants'. The British Bill of Rights could be better tailored to the needs of citizens in twenty-first-century Britain.	The European Convention on Human Rights may be old but this also means that it is a tried and tested piece of legislation. It was written in a different era but its provisions are sufficiently flexible to allow for the granting of new rights not considered by those who drafted the document, for example, the right of mixed-sex couples who do not wish to marry to form civil partnerships. Civil partnerships had previously only been available to same-sex couples.
A key aim of any British Bill of Rights would be to reduce the number of human rights cases that reach the courts. The smaller number of cases would allow important cases to be heard more quickly. It would also be good for the taxpayer. Many human rights cases are funded through legal aid and this means that the government uses tax revenue to pay a person's legal costs. Reducing the number of cases would decrease the legal aid bill.	Reducing the number of human rights cases is unnecessary because the number that reach the courts is already small. Only 25% of cases that reach the Supreme Court involve any aspect of human rights law, and sometimes this is not the main focus of the case.

Arguments for the British Bill of Rights	Arguments against the British Bill of Rights
The introduction of the 'permission stage' into the legal process would be a key mechanism for ensuring that fewer human rights cases reached the courts, with judges only hearing cases that concerned serious breaches of human rights. This would free up court time, which matters because there is currently a considerable backlog of cases. The smaller number of cases would move more quickly through the courts and this would provide faster access to justice.	The introduction of a permission stage would create an additional hurdle for those who wanted to bring human rights cases. Requiring people to have their human rights claim judged sufficiently serious before they could bring it to court may deter some people with valid claims from pursuing them. If the permission stage is not sufficiently well administered it may lead to people being denied the right to bring claims that would stand a good chance of success if they came before the courts.
At present, the right to trial by jury is only guaranteed for those accused of serious criminal offences. Over 90% of criminal cases are tried without a jury, either because they are heard in magistrates' courts or because the defendant has pleaded guilty. A British Bill of Rights that guaranteed the right to trial by jury would uphold the rule of law and bring Britain into line with other liberal democracies, including Australia, Canada, the United States and New Zealand.	As its name suggests, a British Bill of Rights would be aimed primarily at safeguarding British citizens. Dominic Raab, the Lord Chancellor who oversaw the production of the 2022 British Bill of Rights, stated that 'all UK citizens should be able to enjoy the same legal protections'. This falls short of a commitment to upholding universal human rights and may mean that immigrants find themselves disadvantaged in the British courts.
The Conservatives have made it clear that a key aim of any British Bill of Rights would be to make it easier to deport non-British nationals with criminal convictions from the UK. This would make the country safer for British citizens. The Conservative Party argues that this measure could be very important in protecting people from the threat of terrorism.	As long as the UK remains part of the European Court of Human Rights, individuals will still be able to make human rights claims there. This is not a perfect solution because taking a case to the court in Strasbourg is a lengthy and expensive process. It is normal for there to be a 3-year gap between a case being lodged at the court and a verdict given on that case. The time and costs of going to Strasbourg rule this out as an option for most people. The Human Rights Act, by enabling British courts to judge cases, widened access to justice. The British Bill of Rights could narrow that access again especially if it took the step of withdrawing Britain from the European Court of Human Rights.

Arguments for the British Bill of Rights	Arguments against the British Bill of Rights
The power of newspaper owners and editors in British political life is such that any future human rights legislation is likely to retain the commitment given in the 2022 bill to strengthening press freedom. This would be good for the country as a whole. A free press is a key aspect of liberal democracy, not least because of the role the media play in holding parliament and the government to account for their actions.	The proposal to offer lower levels of compensation to those with criminal convictions is also likely to remain part of any future bill. Conservatives support this because they believe that it is important to be tough on law and order. The Labour Party and human rights groups, such as Liberty, would oppose such a move because it suggests that some people are more deserving of human rights than others. They argue that people whose rights have been abused should be treated equally regardless of their past behaviour.

Box 2.3 Key definition

Rule of law: the principle that the law should apply equally to all people

Conclusion

Both those who support and those who oppose the introduction of a British Bill of Rights agree that it would make important changes to the way human rights law operates in the United Kingdom. The scale and precise nature of any future bill's impact cannot be predicted but it will inspire plenty of discussion in the media. Following this discussion will prove instructive for all students of politics.

Exam success

The Human Rights Act is a controversial piece of legislation. Even many of its supporters acknowledge that it provides imperfect protection of human rights. Its opponents argue that the rights it has granted to individuals and minorities have sometimes undermined the safety of wider society. Questions in this area may be framed as follows:

- *Evaluate the view that the Human Rights Act provides the best possible protection of rights and freedoms in the UK.* (Edexcel style, 30 marks)
- *'The Human Rights Act provides the best possible protection of rights and freedoms in the UK.' Analyse and evaluate this statement.* (AQA style, 30 marks)

The best responses will not only evaluate the Human Rights Act but also consider other ways in which rights and freedoms in the UK could be protected. Essays should consider the following:

- The Human Rights Act allows people living in the UK to claim a whole range of rights and freedoms. These include the rights to life and liberty and freedom of thought, conscience, religion, expression and assembly. Court cases brought under the Human Rights Act have allowed people to defend rights the government wished to deny them. For example, in the case of AA v Secretary of State for the Home Department, convicted drug dealer AA was allowed to remain in the UK, against the wishes of the home secretary.

- The Human Rights Act is an Act of Parliament and under the doctrine of parliamentary sovereignty could be repealed at any time. An entrenched bill of rights within a codified constitution would provide better protection for rights and freedoms because it could not be repealed by a simple majority vote in parliament.
- The European Convention on Human Rights, which the Human Rights Act incorporates into British law, is 70 years old and could be considered unfit for purpose in the twenty-first century because, for example, it provides no guaranteed protection for LGBTQ+ rights.
- Judicial interpretations made under the terms of the Human Rights Act could be said to have extended rights to those not deserving of them, at the expense of wider society. For example, in the 2006 Afghan Hijackers case, judges ruled that a group of Afghan men who had hijacked an aeroplane to travel to the UK should be allowed to stay in this country despite the criminal method they had used to travel here.

What next?

Read:

- 'A UK Bill of Rights', Tom Hickman, *London Review of Books*, Volume 44, Number 6, 24 March 2022 (www.lrb.co.uk).
- 'British privacy law now rivals libel law in gagging the press', *The Economist*, 19 February 2022 (www.economist.com).
- 'Bill of Rights to strengthen freedom of speech and curb bogus human rights claims', 22 June 2022 (www.gov.uk).
- 'Explainer: Liberty's Guide to the government's plan to "overhaul" the Human Rights Act', 7 March 2022 (www.libertyhumanrights.org.uk).

Chapter 3

Political parties: are the Liberal Democrats re-emerging as a political force?

Focus

Examination specifications require students to understand the reasons behind voting behaviour and electoral outcomes. These include parties' policies and manifestos and their campaign strategies, as well as the context within which elections are conducted. Both AQA and Edexcel specify that students must have knowledge of the history and development of the Liberal Democrat Party.

Edexcel	UK Politics 2.2 and 4.1	Established political parties Voting behaviour and the media
AQA	3.1.2.2 and 3.1.2.3	Elections and referendums Political parties

Context

In 2010 the Liberal Democrats were junior partners in a coalition government with the Conservatives, but from 2015–20 the party appeared to be in a state of terminal decline. In the 2010 general election, the Liberal Democrats won 57 seats. In 2015 they were reduced to just 8 seats. 2015 was also the year in which the Liberal Democrats lost their position as the third biggest party in parliament to the Scottish National Party. The elections of 2017 and 2019 were little better for the Liberal Democrats. Although they remained the third biggest party in terms of vote share, they won only 12 parliamentary seats in 2017 and 11 in 2019.

In the last 2 years the Liberal Democrats have had more to celebrate. They have achieved three by-election wins, all in what had been considered to be safe Conservative seats. By-elections are held when a seat in the House of Commons falls vacant because of the death or resignation of an MP. The first Liberal Democrat by-election win was in Chesham and Amersham in June 2021, the second in North Shropshire in December 2021 and the third in June 2022 in Tiverton and Honiton. 2022 also saw the Liberal Democrats make considerable gains in the local council elections. Do these results mark the start of a longer-term improvement in fortunes for the Liberal Democrats or are they just temporary successes?

Chapter 3

Liberal Democrat by-election wins, 2021–22

Case study 3.1: Chesham and Amersham, June 2021

The Conservative MP for Chesham and Amersham, Cheryl Gillan, died in April 2021. She had held the seat since 1992 and it had been a safe one for the Conservatives since its creation in 1974. At the June 2021 by-election, the Conservatives found their vote share reduced to just 35.5%, down from the 55.4% Gillan had achieved in 2019. The Liberal Democrats increased their percentage of the vote from 26.3% in 2019 to 56.7% after a high-profile campaign by Sarah Green. The Green Party came third in the by-election, pushing Labour into fourth place with just 1.6% of the vote.

Case study 3.2: North Shropshire, December 2021

This by-election followed the resignation from the House of Commons of Conservative MP Owen Paterson in November 2021. Paterson resigned after the Parliamentary Commissioner for Standards found that he had acted improperly in using his position as MP to try to advance the interests of two companies for which he worked as a paid consultant. At the 2019 election, Paterson had won 62.7% of the vote in this very safe Conservative seat and the Labour candidate had won 22.1%. The Liberal Democrats had come in third place, with a 10% vote share. At the by-election, successful Liberal Democrat candidate Helen Morgan achieved a swing of 27.2% to win the seat. The Conservatives fought hard to retain North Shropshire but Labour ran a quiet campaign. Labour denied that their low-key approach was intended to help the Liberal Democrats but left-leaning newspaper the *Guardian* used an editorial on 6 December to encourage Labour supporters in North Shropshire to vote Liberal Democrat in the by-election.

Case study 3.3: Honiton and Tiverton, June 2022

The seat of Honiton and Tiverton was left vacant by the resignation of Neil Parish, who stood down as a member of parliament after admitting to watching pornography in the House of Commons chamber. Honiton and Tiverton was considered to be one of the safest Conservative seats in the country. It was a seat the Conservatives had won by a large majority in all elections since 1997, and the gap between the Conservatives and the party in second place had widened in every election since 2010. In the 2019 election, Parish had won 62.2% of the votes, 40 percentage points ahead of his nearest rival, Labour's Liz Pole. A Liberal Democrat win in this by-election was by no means certain. The Conservatives picked a strong candidate, the deputy mayor for Honiton, Helen Hurford. She ran a campaign in which she distanced herself from her party, not mentioning the Conservatives in some of her election publicity, for example. As in North Shropshire, the Liberal Democrats were helped by Labour keeping its campaigning to a minimum. The final result, which saw Liberal Democrat candidate Richard Foord win 52.2% of the vote to Helen Hurford's 38.5%, shocked many in the Conservative Party who had expected to narrowly retain the seat.

What factors explain the recent Liberal Democrat success in by-elections?

The Liberal Democrats have a history of by-election success. From Eastbourne in 1910 to Brent East in 2003 and Brecon and Radnorshire in 2019, the Liberal Democrats have shown that they can bring about substantial swings in parliamentary seats previously held by the Conservative or Labour parties. The three recent by-election wins confirm this pattern.

There are several reasons why the Liberal Democrats do well in by-elections. The first thing working in their favour is that they are many voters' second choice. Committed Labour voters tend to prefer the Liberal Democrats to the Conservatives, and instinctive Conservative voters find the Liberal Democrats preferable to Labour. This means that at by-elections the Liberal Democrats can win over voters more naturally inclined to support one of the major parties. The major parties find it harder to persuade voters to switch sides. Furthermore, in the 2019 election, the Liberal Democrats came second in 91 constituencies. Chesham and Amersham was one of these. Winning these seats is less of a challenge for the Liberal Democrats than for the parties placed third in those constituencies because they start from a stronger position.

Neither of these factors is sufficient to explain Liberal Democrat success, particularly not in North Shropshire or Tiverton and Honiton, two seats in which the Liberal Democrats lagged in third place in 2019. The strategies the Liberal Democrats use when fighting by-elections are also key. They try to choose people connected to the local area as their candidates. Richard Foord was already living in Devon when he was selected to fight the seat of Tiverton and Honiton. Voters appreciate candidates they feel understand the local area and its people. As a former army officer, who had won medals for military service in the Balkans and the war in Iraq, Foord was also well placed to appeal to typical Conservative voters, who tend to credit those who have had military careers with a high level of patriotism (love for their country). A belief in the importance of the British nation is a conservative value.

The campaigns the Liberal Democrats fight tend to be local ones, focusing on specific issues they know matter to voters in the area. This strategy ensures that their campaigning seems realistic and their promises achievable. The local focus also avoid an emphasis on national issues over which voters know they have little influence in parliament. In the Chesham and Amersham by-election of 2021, Liberal Democrat candidate Sarah Green ran on a platform of opposing the High Speed 2 rail link that will run through the constituency and rejecting changes to planning laws that would have seen more houses built in Amersham and Chesham. Both the rail link and the proposed planning changes were unpopular across political divides in Chesham and Amersham. Speaking out against them won Green support from voters who had backed both the Conservatives and Labour in the past. Helen Morgan, Liberal Democrat candidate for the 2021 by-election in North Shropshire employed a similar approach in her campaigning.

She emphasised that she wanted to improve local healthcare provision and provide more practical support for the farmers who were a significant community within North Shropshire.

Liberal Democrat supporters are encouraged to play a very active role in by-election campaigns by delivering leaflets and speaking with voters. This is intended not just to raise the profile of the party but also to show voters that they care. When polling day is close, the party brings in activists from across the country to boost the Liberal Democrat presence and ensure a flurry of last minute campaigning. This makes the party appear popular, which can help persuade undecided voters that backing the Liberal Democrats will not be a wasted vote.

The Conservative and Labour parties have more supporters than the Liberal Democrats but do not always tend to mobilise them to the same extent, perhaps because they believe that their higher national profile will be sufficient to win votes. The Liberal Democrats have a smaller national-level profile so make this extra local effort work to their advantage.

Why did voters turn to the Liberal Democrats in the 2022 local council elections?

The local council elections of 2022 were a cause for celebration among Liberal Democrats. They did far better than predicted, winning 868 council seats in total, 224 more than they had held previously. They won control of a number of councils, including Hull, which had been held by the Labour Party, and Woking and Gosport, both of which had been Conservative-led. The Liberal Democrats also did well in newly formed council areas, such as Somerset, where they gained 37 of the 61 seats. Their successful defence of all 11 councils where they were already in charge made them the only party to retain control in all areas they had held prior to this round of elections.

One reason why the Liberal Democrats did so well in local council elections is their low profile at Westminster. Unlike the Conservative and Labour parties, they were not held to account for their national policies or leadership. This allowed the Liberal Democrats to focus on local issues, where they could show a proven track record of success. In North Bedfordshire, for example, Liberal Democrats emphasised their record of fixing potholes in local roads. Attacks on other parties also centred around local issues. In Hull, the Liberal Democrats were very critical of unpopular policies pursued by the Labour party, particularly their decision to increase the number of bus and cycle lanes in the city, which had reduced the road space available for other vehicles, and was much disliked by car drivers. Liberal Democrats across the country kept their achievements and campaigns at the forefront of voters' minds through printed bulletins, which they updated every 6 weeks. The presence of a local Liberal Democrat MP also seems to have translated into success in council elections, with the party making gains in eight of the areas where they have a sitting MP, including Kingston-upon-Thames, Oxford, Richmond-upon-Thames, St Albans and Westmorland.

How significant are the Liberal Democrats' recent successes?

The swings achieved by the Liberal Democrats in their three most recent by-election victories are significant. 290 Conservative MPs hold their seats with a smaller majority than Neil Parish commanded in Honiton and Tiverton. The Liberal Democrat victory there saw them overturning a Conservative majority bigger than any they have reversed in the past. This will give the party confidence but it certainly does not guarantee that they will achieve a strong showing in the next general election.

Tactical voting has helped the Liberal Democrats in their by-election victories. Voters are usually happier to vote tactically at by-elections, when they know that the result will not affect who is in power nationally, than they are at general elections. As importantly, the Liberal Democrats will not be able to maintain their focus on local issues during a general election campaign. The low countrywide profile that has helped them recently will disadvantage them when party leaders and national policies are at the centre of campaigning efforts. The Liberal Democrats also lack the resources and volunteers to run a nationwide campaign with the same intensity that characterises their approach in by-elections.

History suggests that the Liberal Democrats cannot even guarantee to hold the seats they have won in by-elections. The Liberal Democrats won Richmond Park in a by-election in 2016 but lost it again at the 2019 general election. In August 2019, the Liberal Democrats achieved a 12% swing to win the seat of Brecon and Radnorshire at a by-election. They lost the seat again just 4 months later.

A formal electoral pact with the Labour Party could make a significant difference to the Liberal Democrats. If each party agreed not to run a candidate in any constituency they could not win, they would be maximising the other party's chance of success. The Liberal Democrats would, for example, be far more likely to win the 91 constituencies in which they achieved second place in the 2019 election if Labour did not contest these seats. Even an informal agreement between the two parties to hold back in constituencies in which the other party had a better chance of victory would benefit the Liberal Democrats. Left-wing publications such as the *New Statesman* and the *Guardian* have talked up the benefits of such a pact for both parties. Liberal Democrat leader, Ed Davey, hinted in a March 2022 interview with the *Financial Times* that he was open to the idea. The Labour Party are the sticking point. Keir Starmer has publicly ruled out any deal, formal or informal, with the Liberal Democrats.

In the unlikely event that a deal were to be agreed, the Liberal Democrats would face another obstacle to electoral success. Three quarters of the seats in which the Liberal Democrats came second in 2019 were majority leave areas in the 2016 Brexit referendum. The Liberal Democrats might find it hard to win over leave voters, especially when their current policy on Europe is to rejoin the Common Market. That said, 57.8% of voters in Honiton and Tiverton backed Brexit and this did not prevent the constituency falling to the Liberal Democrats in the 2021 by-election.

Exam success

The position of the Liberal Democrat party in UK politics is unsettled. It could be seen as no more than a minor party. It has few seats in the House of Commons and does little to shape current debates about national policy. On the other hand, this chapter has shown that it can win significant electoral successes and compete with the major parties. Questions in this area may be framed as follows:

- *Evaluate the view that the Liberal Democrats are an insignificant electoral and political force in the UK.* (Edexcel style, 30 marks)
- *'The Liberal Democrats are an insignificant electoral and political force in the UK.' Analyse and evaluate this statement.* (AQA style, 25 marks)

The best responses will evaluate the position of the Liberal Democrats relative both to smaller parties in the UK and to the Conservative and Labour parties. Essays should consider the following:

- The recent Liberal Democrat performance in elections. They won 11% of the votes in the 2019 general election, far more than any other minor party. The Liberal Democrats' recent by- and local election success shows that they remain a force to be reckoned with politically. A party that can achieve such large voter swings in by-elections and take seats from the party in government should be considered a significant force electorally. At the time of the last election, the Liberal Democrats came second in 91 constituencies, which also suggests their importance as a political force.
- The Liberal Democrats have only 14 seats in the House of Commons, well behind the third largest party, the SNP, which has 44. This impacts on the extent to which they can influence political debates and scrutinise the executive. Other minor parties have outstripped the Liberal Democrats in their ability to influence politics. For example, the threat from UKIP was partly what prompted David Cameron to call the Brexit referendum, and the SNP has helped to make Scottish independence a live issue.
- Compared to his counterparts in the Conservative and Labour parties, Ed Davey, the leader of the Liberal Democrats, has a low profile in the media and among the general public.

What next?

Read:

- 'The informal Labour–Lib Dem Alliance could doom the Tories', Philip Collins, *New Statesman*, 24 June 2022 (www.newstatesman.com).
- 'The Tories are terrified of a Labour–Lib Dem pact — and they're right to be', Neal Lawson, *Guardian*, 2 May 2022 (www.theguardian.com).
- 'Lib Dems pave the way for pact with Labour to oust the Tories', Jasmine Cameron-Chileshe and George Parker, *Financial Times*, 10 March 2022 (www.ft.com).

Chapter 4

Devolved and divided? The causes and consequences of Northern Ireland's seismic election

Focus

Examination specifications require students to have thorough knowledge and understanding of recent elections in all of the UK's regions and to analyse and evaluate the implications of regional election results for the process of devolution in the United Kingdom.

Edexcel	UK Politics 3.1-3.3	Electoral systems
	UK Government 1.3	Devolution: the Northern Ireland Assembly and Executive
AQA	3.1.2.2	Elections and referendums
	3.1.1.5	Devolution: the Northern Ireland Assembly and Executive

Evaluation of regional election systems and their outcomes will also support analysis of the advantages and disadvantages of the UK's representative democracy (Edexcel topic 1.1 democracy and participation) and the nature of democracy and patterns of participation (AQA topic 3.1.2.1 democracy and participation).

In addition, students need good knowledge of the policies and developments of the UK's minor parties, both to consider the impact of party policies and manifestos on voting (Edexcel topic 4.1 Voting behaviour; AQA topic 3.1.2.3 Elections and referendums) and on the potential development of the UK towards a multi-party system (Edexcel topic 2.4 Political parties; AQA topic 3.1.2.3 Political parties).

Party political developments in Northern Ireland also have significant implications for the ongoing impact and process of devolution in the UK in terms of the role and power of the devolved bodies themselves and the extent to which the constitutional reforms which gave rise to the current devolved arrangements within the UK should be 'taken further' (Edexcel topics 1.3 and 1.4; AQA topic 3.1.1.5).

Finally, students following the US and comparative route will use their knowledge and understanding of the UK's party system to draw comparisons with the party system of the USA (Edexcel comparative topic 6.2.9; AQA comparative topic 3.2.2.4).

Context

In May 2022, elections to choose the Northern Ireland Assembly's 90 members took place – the seventh set of regional elections since the signing of the Good Friday Agreement in 1998. The win for Sinn Fein was widely described as 'historic' and 'seismic', being the first time that a nationalist party had won the most Assembly seats. The 2022 result also pushed the previously dominant Democratic Unionist Party (DUP) into second place and saw the notable rise of a potentially disruptive third party, the cross-community Alliance Party.

Table 4.1 Northern Ireland's main political parties

Party	2022 Assembly seats (90)	Profile	Current party policies
Sinn Fein (founded 1905)	27	Sinn Fein is an Irish Republican party supporting nationalism. It is active throughout the Republic of Ireland and Northern Ireland.	Sinn Fein proposes higher taxes for wealthy individuals and big corporations, and increasing investment in public services, especially investment in housing and social and health care. The party is pro-immigration and takes a more liberal stance on abortion rights in certain circumstances.
Democratic Unionist Party (DUP) (founded 1971)	25	The DUP is Northern Ireland's foremost unionist and loyalist political party in Northern Ireland.	The DUP staunchly defends Northern Ireland's place in the UK, supports 'Britishness' and Ulster Protestant culture against Irish nationalism. The party is seen as right of centre and socially conservative, opposing abortion and same-sex marriage.
Alliance Party (founded 1970)	17	The Alliance Party emerged from the New Ulster Movement with moderate support for unionism. More recently it has restyled itself as neither unionist nor nationalist.	The Alliance Party's neutral stance on unionism, its support for non-sectarian politics and belief in a distinctive Northern Ireland character and community has led to increased popularity in recent years. The party's recent popularity is largely a result of its liberal philosophy, its support of abortion rights, immigration, LGBT rights, and of a combined education system where Catholics and Protestants are educated together.

Party	2022 Assembly seats (90)	Profile	Current party policies
The Ulster Unionist Party (UUP) (founded 1905)	9	For generations, the UUP was the leading force in the unionist politics of Northern Ireland. It was instrumental in the signing of the Northern Ireland Agreement but has recently been 'eclipsed' by the rise of the DUP.	The UUP has suffered a leaching of support to the 'harder line' DUP and been set back by high profile defections of senior representatives to the DUP in recent years. Long seen as the more moderate force for unionism, the party has struggled to establish a distinctive foothold and its loss of support in Northern Ireland is echoed at Westminster where it has not returned an MP since 2010.
Social Democrat and Labour party (SDLP) (founded 1970)	8	One of the driving forces for peace in Northern Ireland, the SDLP sits on the left of and is affiliated to the Labour party.	The SDLP advocates a united Ireland through Irish reunification and campaigns for the further devolution of powers while Northern Ireland remains in the UK. However, Republican supporters have shifted steadily to Sinn Fein, which has been the most popular nationalist party for more than 20 years. The party remains a strong supporter of traditional, rural and agricultural communities, seeking enhanced environmental standards and opposing Brexit.

Beneath the headline-grabbing triumph of Sinn Fein, the magnitude of the result was a little more qualified. In fact, Sinn Fein won exactly the same number of seats as 5 years before in 2017. The root cause of its win lay instead in the DUP's modest but critical loss of three seats, thereby handing the balance of power in the Northern Ireland Assembly to Sinn Fein.

Months of governing paralysis followed the vote. While the DUP refused to participate in government until post-Brexit trading arrangements (the Northern Ireland Protocol) were addressed, Sinn Fein's leader Michelle O'Neill referred to such protests as 'cover' for preventing an Irish nationalist becoming first minister. However, the threat of another election in December 2022 was averted when Northern Ireland Secretary Chris Heaton-Harris reversed his own threat, issued to force the parties to work together.

For many commentators, the election results raised more questions over the future of the region under a nationalist party than answers.

> **Box 4.1** **Key definitions**
>
> **The Good Friday Agreement:** signed in April 1998 and approved by voters through referendums in May 1998, the agreement was one of the most significant developments in Northern Ireland's peace process. It was a cross-party agreement between most of Northern Ireland's political parties and the British and Irish governments to create a devolved system of government in the region and to clarify the relationship between Northern Ireland, the Republic of Ireland and the United Kingdom.
>
> **The Northern Ireland Assembly:** often referred to by the name of its building, Stormont, this is Northern Ireland's unicameral legislature. The Assembly comprises 90 members elected under the Single Transferable Vote (STV) form of proportional representation and selects most of the ministers of the **Northern Ireland Executive** using the principle of power sharing to ensure that unionists and nationalists participate in governing the region according to their levels of support among the electorate.

Victory for Sinn Fein — and a reversal of Northern Ireland's founding rationale?

As widely predicted in the months preceding the vote, the Irish nationalist party duly won the most seats – 27 of the 90 available. The Democratic Unionist Party (DUP)'s loss of three seats, down from 28 in 2017, pushed them into second place and was the largest contributory factor in Sinn Fein's victory. The cross-community Alliance party came third, more than doubling its seats' total to 17.

Sinn Fein's 2022 winning electoral performance was twofold as the party secured the most first preference votes and the most Assembly seats. In 2017, Sinn Fein had polled around 1,000 first preference votes fewer than its main unionist rival and won one seat fewer. In 2022, the party received 66,000 more first preference votes than the DUP, its nearest rival.

Table 4.2 The Northern Ireland Assembly results: votes and seats

Party	Votes			Seats	
	Number	Of total (%)	Change	Count	Change
Sinn Fein	250,388	29.02	↑ 1.1%	27	–
DUP	184,002	21.33	↓ 6.7%	25	↓ 3
Alliance	116,681	13.53	↑ 4.5%	17	↑ 9
Ulster Unionist	96,390	11.17	↓ 1.7%	9	↓ 1
SDLP	78,237	9.07	↓ 2.9%	8	↓ 4
TUV	65,788	7.63	↑ 5.0%	1	–
Green (NI)	16,433	1.90	↓ 0.4%	0	↓ 2
Independent	25,315	2.93	↑ 1.1%	2	↑ 1
Total	862,703	100		90	

The election also marked the first time that a nationalist party — one committed to the reunification of Ireland — had won the most seats. For many commentators, the irony of such an outcome in the centenary year of the 'birth' of Northern

Ireland was not lost. As reviewed on LSE's British Politics and Policy blog, the 'novel political entity' of Northern Ireland had been 'forged to secure an Ulster unionist and Protestant demographic and electoral majority'. Yet the May 2022 result revealed that it 'no longer has either'.

Box 4.2 The birth of Northern Ireland

Centuries of British domination, or Home Rule, was fiercely opposed by the majority of Ireland's Catholic population. At the start of the twentieth century, the gathering strength and organisation of the nationalist movement led Sinn Fein to defy the British and to declare the birth of an Irish Republic in 1919. Facing the prospect of civil war, and attempting to satisfy supporters of the union in the northeast of Ireland, the British government passed the Government of Ireland Act (1920) which set up two parliaments and partitioned the island into north and south.

Opposition to this partition saw Sinn Fein proclaim Ireland as the Irish Free State in 1922. Within a day, and in accordance with the Government of Ireland Act, six of the nine counties of Ulster withdrew from the new Republic, and accepted self-government within the United Kingdom. The electoral prospects of this new territory of Northern Ireland were carefully calculated to all but guarantee continued Ulster unionist support from a considerable Protestant majority.

Sinn Fein in the Republic of Ireland

In the Republic of Ireland Sinn Fein's history is more that of an outsider party, only relatively recently making electoral gains by winning 37 of the 157 seats in the 2020 Irish general election. The party now appears as an increasingly viable alternative to the two parties that have dominated Irish politics for generations in coalitions – Fianna Fail and Fine Gael. The two main parties are increasingly associated with policy failure, especially over housing and social policy for younger voters, which Sinn Fein is untarnished by. Sinn Fein's left-leaning stance is supported by a growing number of younger and middle-aged voters attracted by the party's commitments to higher public spending on housing, health and social care.

The passing of time has also allowed for greater distance to be placed between Sinn Fein and the terrorist activities of the IRA. Polls increasingly indicate that younger voters are less troubled by traditional links between the party and Republican violence, seeing instead the opportunities and possibilities of a united Ireland.

Sinn Fein in Northern Ireland

Under the terms of the Good Friday Agreement, Sinn Fein has long been part of a power-sharing government, though it has distanced itself from many unionist causes by taking up more liberal and progressive stances in supporting abortion and minority rights. Support for Sinn Fein has grown, especially among younger and middle-aged voters, in which it leads the DUP by over 10 percentage points.

Box 4.3 **Age divide over unification**

In recent years, Lord Ashcroft Polls have consistently reported a growing
divide between young and old over the possible unification of Ireland.
Aggregated polls since 2019 indicate that while nearly two-thirds of over-65s
are opposed to the possibility of unification, over 60% of those in the 18–24
bracket are in favour of possible unification.

Source: Lord Ashcroft Polls (www.lordashcroftpolls.com)

Sinn Fein has also used its support to generate enthusiasm for the possibility of
a vote on the unification of Ireland. However the nationalist cause in total has
not significantly prospered. While Sinn Fein retained its 27 (of 90) seats, SDLP,
the other main nationalist party, declined from 12 to 8 seats, with the combined
nationalist first preference vote only just over 41%, behind the total unionist
vote-share. The secretary of state for Northern Ireland is unlikely to interpret
the Assembly elections as signalling a wave of support for Irish unity or for the
holding of a referendum on the question any time soon.

Brexit, voting and the balance of power

While the DUP's first preference vote share declined significantly from 2017
(down from 28.1% to 21.3% in 2022), the party won a seemingly disproportional
number of Assembly seats (nearly 28% of total seats), down just 3 on 2017. The
DUP's seat total was boosted by a larger number of lower preference vote transfers
than Sinn Fein received, making the DUP the main beneficiary of the use of the
proportional Single Transferable Vote (STV) system used.

Box 4.4 **The Northern Ireland voting system**

The system used in Northern Ireland is called the Single Transferable Vote
(STV). It is a form of Proportional Representation (PR) designed to make sure
that candidates elected represent accurately the opinions of the voters.

Every voter has only one vote, but they can ask for it to be transferred from
one candidate to another to make sure it is not wasted. This is done by
numbering the candidates in order of preference 1, 2, 3, 4, 5 and so on instead
of just putting an 'X' against one of them.

Source: Northern Ireland elections at www.nidirect.gov.uk

The DUP's failure to prevent the UK government agreeing to a protocol that saw
Northern Ireland remain subject to the single market and customs rules of the EU
contributed to significant fractures in the party's support base. In 2022, a sizeable
number of unionist supporters cast their votes first for Traditional Unionist
Voice (TUV), the party that backed the hardest line on border proposals and
campaigned with the words 'No Sea Border' next to its name on the ballot paper.

Northern Ireland had suffered decades of bloody conflict until a peace was negotiated in the 1998 Good Friday Agreement. Part of this peace was to have an open border with the Republic of Ireland to the south. When the UK was in the European Union there was friction-free movement of goods between north and south because both sides complied with EU single market rules.

However, the 2016 Brexit referendum threatened to return a hard border, which would anger Republicans and potentially see a return of sectarian violence. The Northern Ireland protocol was drawn up to provide clarity by keeping Northern Ireland in the EU customs union and shifting the bulk of the regulation of the movement of goods to between Northern Ireland and the rest of the UK.

Source: 'Focus on: the Northern Ireland protocol' by Rupert Dexter, *Politics Review*, Volume 32 Issue 1

Many first preference votes for the TUV were followed by lower-order votes cast for the DUP. Yet TUV candidates received very few lower order votes from those who had voted for other unionist parties' candidates first. So while the TUV won 7.6% of first preference votes, the party received just one seat (returning only its party leader).

Even boosted by lower order votes, the result for the DUP was severely disappointing, occurring less than 3 years since the party had held the balance of power in Westminster in support of Theresa May's otherwise minority Conservative government. For some commentators though, the result was seen as a bottoming out in support for the DUP, after a very difficult and acrimonious few years that have been over-shadowed by seemingly endless negotiations and stand-offs over the trade arrangements with the South and the UK. In electoral terms, the pressure on the DUP's right from the TUV, and on its liberal left from the UUP, was far more fierce than that faced by Sinn Fein for its traditional vote share, yet the DUP's vote held up comparatively well.

Trouble began almost immediately as DUP leader Sir Jeffrey Donaldson maintained that his party would not engage in negotiations to form a government until his party's concerns about the post-Brexit trading arrangements contained in the Northern Ireland Protocol were resolved.

Box 4.6 DUP condemned for 'paralysing Stormont'

The Democratic Unionist party (DUP) was condemned by political leaders in Northern Ireland for 'paralysing the Stormont assembly and executive in a dramatic escalation of the party's campaign against the Northern Ireland protocol'.

Sinn Fein and other parties in Northern Ireland described the move as 'shameful' and 'disgraceful' and said it treated voters with contempt.

For the DUP, it was a 'message to Downing Street and the EU that the DUP is willing to create a destabilising vacuum in Northern Ireland to secure changes to the protocol, which puts post-Brexit checks on goods entering the region from Great Britain'.

Source: 'DUP condemned for paralysing Stormont as protocol row deepens', *Guardian*, 13 May 2022

The rise of Alliance — a cross-community future for Northern Ireland politics?

Where once existed an almost complete void between nationalist and unionist voting blocs, Alliance has latterly prospered, championing the possibility for a sea-change to what many, younger Northern Irish voters perceive as a stagnant and unnecessarily binary party political system.

In terms of the May 2022 vote, lower-order transfers from almost all parties — from 'soft nationalist' and 'soft unionist' supporters of the main parties, from the SDLP and the UUP — led to substantial electoral gains for Alliance and subsequent perceptions of its over-representation in the Assembly. Alliance won just 13.5% of first preference votes, but won 17 seats (18.8%), more than doubling its seat-share compared to 2017.

'Neutrality' on the future of Northern Ireland within the UK was until very recently considered an electoral liability, but with younger voters added to the electorate year-on-year, it could prove to be Alliance's biggest electoral asset.

Box 4.7 **Rise of Alliance reveals surprising facets of the North's shifting politics**

As the third-largest party in any new Assembly, Alliance has now 'become a major force in the North's political landscape' but, in so doing, has raised a crucial question: 'what does it say about the direction of political travel in contemporary Northern Ireland?' The answer appears to lie within voters who declare themselves to be 'neither' nationalist not unionist.

The annual Northern Ireland Life and Times (NILT) survey has recorded the 'steady if fluctuating growth of this 'neither' community from 33% of respondents in 1998 (first year of the survey) to 42% in the most recent data of 2020'. They are numbers that indicate significant potential for future growth for a party such as Alliance. Added to this, 'data from NILT show that almost 38% of those who identify as 'neither' claimed to support the Alliance Party, a significant way ahead of both the SDLP and the Greens, who were both on 11% of respondents'.

Source: 'Rise of Alliance reveals surprising facets of North's shifting politics', *The Irish Times*, 17 May 2022

It is not just the nationalist/unionist centre ground that Alliance appears to be catering for. Viewed as a socially liberal party, campaigning for marriage equality, women's rights, an integrated education system, reforms to end the nationalist/unionist label that dominates the political system, commentators watch with serious interest as to whether 2022's gains can herald a genuinely new phase in the politics of Northern Ireland.

Comparisons and connections

The May elections in Northern Ireland were accompanied by other votes that had significant consequences and impact on party support and party systems in the UK.

Local elections

Boris Johnson's premiership came to its own conclusion a few months later, but the local elections in England in May 2022 provided evidence to the Conservative Party that Johnson's electoral allure was over.

Prior to May, the Conservative Party held 39% of council seats in the UK and 42% in England. In May 2022, the party lost around 500 council seats and lost control of 11 councils — most worryingly in 'blue wall' areas such as Huntingdonshire, Maidstone and Wokingham.

Labour on the other hand made gains outside London and in Scotland, and its vote held up in many northern 'Leave' supporting areas that had been so devastating for the Party in both the 2019 general election and the local elections in 2021.

The Liberal Democrats made notable gains in Somerset and Surrey and are said to be shaping up for an electoral recovery in the mid 2020s.

UK party systems

A further important way that the politics of Northern Ireland can be explored within examination questions is to use the electoral data, election outcomes and party support as part of the evaluation and analysis required to respond to questions on the extent to which the UK remains a two-party system or has seen sufficient electoral turbulence to support a multi-party conclusion.

In the post-war era, Labour and the Conservatives dominated electoral politics across the UK. In the 1951 general election, won by Winston Churchill's Conservative Party, the two main parties shared nearly 97% of the votes between them. Nearly 70 years later however, while the two main parties still dominate, their combined vote share reduced to 75% in 2019 and their domination of seats is largely confined to England, rather than the UK as a whole.

That said, while Labour and the Conservatives still win over 85% of the available seats in the House of Commons (nearly 90% in the 2017 general election), nationalist parties routinely dominate Westminster and devolved assembly seats in Scotland and Northern Ireland.

The use of alternative voting systems in non-Westminster elections has undoubtedly helped minor parties to convert votes to seats far more effectively. In Scotland, the Scottish Nationalist Party (SNP) has moved from minor party status in the Scottish Parliament (winning 35 seats to Labour's 56 in 1999) to become the predominant, governing party for a decade.

What next?

Research: the full briefing file on the result in Northern Ireland Assembly Elections: 2022 (**https://commonslibrary.parliament.uk/research-briefings/cbp-9549**).

Review: the LSE's full report on the election, 'Much more than meh: The 2022 Northern Ireland Assembly Elections' (**https://blogs.lse.ac.uk/2022-northern-ireland-assembly-elections**).

Chapter 5

The constitution: is the UK's uncodified constitution working?

Focus

All examination specifications require students to have strong knowledge and understanding of the nature and sources of the UK constitution and of all the major constitutional developments since 1997. The debate over whether the UK constitution 'works' is particularly relevant, leading to evaluation of whether reforms should be taken forward and whether the UK's constitutional arrangements should be codified.

Edexcel	UK Government 1.4	Debates on further constitutional reform
AQA	3.1.1.1	Issues and debates around recent constitutional changes

Context

In the summer of 2022, the UK was portrayed by many commentators as hurtling towards further political turmoil following the loss of confidence in Boris Johnson as prime minister (see chapter 7) — the latest in a seemingly endless cycle of constitutional confusion and uncertainty. For a state that has long cherished its internal stability, the turbulence that followed the Brexit referendum, general elections that failed to deliver a secure government, prime ministerial resignations and judicial spats have all served to undermine this. Each crisis is almost invariably accompanied by calls for the UK to reorganise its political and governing arrangements by codifying them into one clear and plainly understood document. The continued informal reliance on elected officials behaving responsibly, goes the argument, will surely lead to a crisis too big to be muddled through.

To emphasise the UK constitution's informal arrangements, *The Atlantic* ran a story by Tom McTague in July 2022 that caught the eye. In it there was acknowledgement that 'in times of crisis, Britain's arcane constitution seems absurd' with reflection on what might have happened if Boris Johnson, instead of resigning, had simply asked the queen to dissolve a parliament that no longer supported him. 'At this point,' mused McTague, 'somebody is sure to cite some old but meaningful convention, only for somebody else to discover that the source of this apparently sacred but largely forgotten rule is in fact an anonymous letter written to a newspaper.' Of course, this is precisely what happened.

Yet in truth, the 2022 resignations of both Boris Johnson and Liz Truss and the process of electing their successors, under rules involving Conservative MPs and party members drawn up by the 1922 Committee, proved to be relatively well mannered and widely accepted transitions from one political head of state to the next. Ultimately, neither Boris Johnson nor Liz Truss were supported by their parliamentary parties to continue in office. Both were required to step down to allow the next most suitable leader to take their places. Far from chaotic, many would argue that the process demonstrated the UK's constitutional arrangements at their most efficient.

So, while students of politics could be forgiven for looking at events in the UK over recent years and seeing a constitution that provides insufficient clarity, little restraint and unsatisfactory guidance when needed most, there are alternative perspectives that portray the UK's constitutional arrangements in a much more positive light.

Box 5.1   Key definitions

The 1922 Committee: a Conservative Party committee made up of all the party's backbenchers. It provides a channel of communication between the parliamentary party and the leadership. The committee's elected chair is the returning officer and presides over leadership elections.

Constitutional codification: refers to the organising of governing arrangements into a single authoritative document setting out the rules and relationships within the state between the governing branches (executive, legislature and judiciary) and between the state and its citizens.

Box 5.2   Does the UK's current constitution still work?

The Institute for Government confirmed that while the question is 'complex', the need to find an answer is 'urgent'. It emphasised that 'leaving the EU has destabilised relationships between the executive, judiciary, and parliament' and, along with the varied responses to the pandemic across regions with devolved responsibilities, has stretched relationships between the nations within the UK too. That said, perhaps the biggest constitutional issue for the Institute for Government is what to do about 'parliament's difficulty in holding the government to account'.

Source: Institute for Government's 'Review of the UK constitution'
(www.instituteforgovernment.org.uk)

Arguments in favour of retaining the UK's current constitutional arrangements

Many states have struggled with the economic difficulties, social upheavals and health-crisis related uncertainties of recent years but throughout this, the UK has shown more often than not that it is underpinned by functioning and effective constitutional principles.

In spite of the serious political and governing difficulties common to many states, the UK has demonstrated that it:

- respects democratic outcomes however undesirable they may be to the government of the day
- allows for the peaceful transfer of power from one administration to the next without violence or serious conflict
- is sufficiently flexible to consider, enact and review constitutional alternatives.

While often taken for granted in the UK, these factors reflect levels of constitutional restraint and responsibility that are both impressive and, many would argue, unique.

1 Respect for democratic outcomes

In the run up to 2014, the Scottish National Party (SNP) was predominant in Scotland indicating that for a number of years, voters had supported a party that was committed to achieving an independent Scotland. The UK government agreed to the holding of a referendum, the result of which could have dissolved the United Kingdom, yet it guaranteed to respect the result. In 2022, the proposal to hold another independence referendum was submitted through the appropriate legal channels.

Comparisons are often drawn with Spain where pro-independence Catalan leaders felt compelled to circumvent legal routes to independence and were imprisoned for sedition and disobedience in 2017 for defying the refusal of the Spanish government to engage in dialogue about a Catalonian independence referendum.

2 Peaceful transition of power

Momentum behind the holding of a referendum about the UK's membership of the EU led to its inclusion in the Conservative Party's 2015 manifesto. David Cameron was the prime minister who called — and subsequently lost — the 2016 vote. Cameron stood down, to be replaced by Theresa May who committed to deliver the result. When May struggled to maintain support for her approach, she was in turn changed for Boris Johnson in 2019, who delivered Brexit. In 2022 Johnson was replaced by Liz Truss when, post-Brexit, he no longer commanded the support and confidence of his party in parliament. Less than 2 months later in October 2022, Rishi Sunak became the UK's prime minister.

Comparisons could be drawn with Donald Trump who took some time to formally concede (accept) the result of the 2020 US presidential election and was accused of inciting an insurrection in 2021 to thwart the inauguration of his successor.

> ### Box 5.3 A peaceful transition of power
>
> The mainstream media in the US has paid scant attention to the recent changing of the guard in the British government. And yet, given the current state of our politics, we might learn a lot from the peaceful transition of power that just took place, as Boris Johnson left office and Liz Truss was installed as Britain's new prime minister.
>
> Source: 'What a peaceful transition of power looks like', Jeff Schechtman interviews Jesse Norman, 9 September 2022 (https://whowhatwhy.org/podcast)

3 Constitutional evolution and adaption

Codified constitutions are often criticised for being static and inflexible. The UK's uncodified arrangements allow for governing arrangements to be adapted over time to better suit or respond to the wishes of citizens. The fact that there are no entrenched constitutional arrangements — no specially protected parts of the UK's governing structures — means that anything can be changed with a simple Act of Parliament. Examples of recent constitutional innovations include:

- Where once referendums were considered 'alien to our traditions' and too often 'the instruments of Nazism and fascism' (Clement Attlee) they are now a firm feature of the UK's democratic make-up. Local referendums have taken place in cities such as Birmingham, Manchester and Edinburgh on issues such as congestion charging; regional referendums have supported greater powers for devolved governments; UK-wide referendums have been held on the UK's electoral system (2011) and Brexit (2016).
- The Fixed-term Parliament Act (2011) sought to put parliament on a similar 'fixed-term' footing to that of the USA. While it negated the ability of a prime minister to call a general election to suit party-political circumstances, it was scrapped in 2021 because it failed to foresee the continuation of a government that could not control the Commons.
- The Human Rights Act (1998) enshrined the European Convention on Human Rights into British domestic law to better protect rights. In 2022, debate centred upon whether this should be replaced with a British Bill of Rights (see chapter 2).

From the creation of devolved governments, a UK Supreme Court and elected mayors, to the introduction of alternative electoral systems and reforms to the House of Lords, the UK's constitution has adapted to move with the times. Arrangements are permanently evolving to reflect a democratic system that is not forever bound by hallowed texts that often lack clarity and relevance.

Arguments for reforming the UK's constitutional arrangements

While there is little doubt that major constitutional changes have occurred, the death of Queen Elizabeth II prompted many commentators to consider the distinct possibility that momentum for radical change might prove to be irresistible. Indeed historian Linda Colley asked in the *New York Times* in September 2022 whether 'the queen's death and the accession of a less popular Charles III [will] contribute to increased levels of turmoil and lead to unstoppable pressure for radical constitutional change, even a new British constitution?'

Box 5.4 Inadequate and insufficient

Linda Colley commented in the *New York Times* that while the UK's institutions of government have undergone change, 'the change has been partial and sometimes inadequately thought out. Power has been devolved away from London, but not sufficiently or systematically so'. For example, while Wales, Scotland and Northern Ireland have their own democratically elected representative bodies, 'England — the largest of the four component parts of the United Kingdom — has no separate assembly of its own, and this has helped to stoke a resentful, inward-looking English nationalism'. In addition, creating a parliament in Edinburgh 'has not... succeeded in defusing separatist sentiment in Scotland, while the Northern Ireland Assembly is currently stalled and nationalist sentiment is rising in Wales'.

Source: 'The radical constitutional change Britain needs',
Linda Colley, *New York Times*, 12 September 2022

Many commentators see some fundamental issues with the UK's constitutional arrangements that can only be solved by radical change.

1 Stretching norms and conventions

The lack of codified clarity in times of extreme governing strain or difficulty — such as during a pandemic, or in the wake of a highly divisive referendum result — has meant that scrutiny responsibilities that the legislature may once have taken in its stride are far less effective in the face of an assertive, forceful executive branch using emergency powers to tackle a crisis. In particular, the passing of significant pieces of Brexit and Covid-19 legislation via delegated legislation with little scrutiny, has meant that MPs 'are not providing effective oversight of major changes in these and other areas' (Institute for Government).

Box 5.5 The 'good chaps' theory of government

The Institute for Government explains that the norms and conventions of the UK's uncodified constitution 'are being pushed to their limits — and sometimes beyond'. They cite the 'absence of clear legal rules' and the fact that the constitution relies on 'a shared understanding of what constitutes good behaviour in public and political life'. The entire basis of the UK's constitutional arrangements is 'trust that people in positions of power will abide by that understanding'. It is something that the constitutional historian Peter Hennessy refers to as 'the "good chaps" theory of government'.

Source: 'The failure of "good chaps": are norms and conventions still working
in the UK constitution?', Institute for Government video, March 2022 (www.youtube.com)

2 Declining parliamentary scrutiny

While a quarter of a century of constitutional reforms has touched almost all areas of UK government and politics, one prominent area has been left untouched. The lack of reform of the Westminster Parliament and the growing powers of the prime minister, developing a more presidential, less accountable style, has seen conflict and struggle between the branches of government — parliament, the government and the courts — reach an all-time high.

The Constitutional Law Matters project is an initiative of the Centre for Public Law at the University of Cambridge's Faculty of Law, its role being to evaluate whether the UK constitution is (still) fit for purpose. The organisation sees a central feature of Boris Johnson's tenure in Number 10 and of post-Brexit political activity in general, as a decline in the parliamentary procedures that support effective levels of scrutiny. It cites the Elections Bill that sought to 'bring the Electoral Commission's strategy and policy under government control' in a bid to 'reduce the Commission's independence and increasing the government's influence and power over the election process'.

3 Disconnection between citizens and state

While the real or perceived disconnect between rulers and people has been on a course of long-term decline, the influence that the public currently has on the decisions made by government is a democratic concern. According to UCL's Constitution Unit in 2022, 77% questioned in a wide-ranging poll felt they had too little influence over how the UK is governed. Opportunities certainly exist for exploring ambitious ideas for reinvigorating democracy in the UK, such as:

- enhanced digital engagement, using artificial intelligence to crowd-source the ideas of people most affected by policies to help design them
- creating citizens' assemblies to focus on major policy challenges facing the country, to improve the public's engagement and bring decision making closer to the people.

For many, the only viable solution is a complete overhaul of the UK's constitutional arrangements by gathering practical, innovative and robust ideas for reform.

Exam success

A central area for students is the extent to which recent constitutional reforms should be taken further. While this might focus on a particular constitutional theme — such as extending devolved government to England or English regions, fully reforming the UK's second chamber (House of Lords), or creating a British Bill of Rights — it may well require responses to focus instead upon whether the UK should fully codify its constitutional arrangements.

- *Evaluate the extent to which constitutional codification is now essential for the UK.* (Edexcel-style, 30 marks)
- *'Constitutional codification is essential for the UK.' Analyse and evaluate this statement.* (AQA-style, 25 marks)

Students wishing to research their essays during the planning phase would be well advised to review UCL's Constitution Unit, which recently provided a detailed summary in response to the question 'Do we need a written constitution?'

Table 5.1 Do we need a written constitution?

Yes	No
The lack of constitutional clarity has worsened recent political crises in the UK. The relationship between referendums and parliamentary sovereignty is particularly difficult to decipher.	The constitution's flexibility has aided what was an unprecedented political — not constitutional — crisis. Most commentators refute the notion that a written constitution would have made resolving post-Brexit difficulties any easier.
The Human Rights Act does not have the same status as a list of fundamental rights in a codified constitution. The need to entrench rights against arbitrary change is required and could be done with a parliamentary super-majority.	Reforms (for example to the protection of rights) can be made, but are distinct from specific arguments for constitutional reform (which could deliver effective protection of rights just as well as a written constitution could).
The current devolution settlement is badly in need of codifying. A federal arrangement with entrenched protection for devolved responsibilities is the only way to avoid the UK's demise.	Written constitutions do not assist complex governing relationships of today. Too short and they are poor guides (e.g. the US Constitution), too long and they are unusable as a guide (e.g. the South African Constitution).

Source: 'Do we need a written constitution?', The Constitution Unit Blog, 8 January 2020 (https://constitution-unit.com)

What next?

Listen to: the WhoWhatWhy podcast 'What a peaceful transition of power looks like' on the transition of power from Boris Johnson to Liz Truss (whowhatwhy.org).

Read:

- 'Ignore the chaos. Britain's system is working', Tom McTague, *The Atlantic*, 14 July 2022 (theatlantic.com).
- The Institute for Government's 'Review of the UK constitution. Does the UK's current constitution still work?' (www.instituteforgovernment.org.uk).

Watch: 'The failure of "good chaps": are norms and conventions still working in the UK constitution?', Institute for Government video, March 2022 (www.youtube.com).

Chapter 6

Parliament and the prime minister: how did parliament contribute to a prime minister's demise?

Focus

The relationships that exist between the branches of government, especially between the legislature and the executive, are central features of all examination specifications. In particular, the effectiveness of the ways in which parliament scrutinises the prime minister, and the various ways in which that scrutiny can be limited or constrained, are essential areas of evaluation.

Edexcel	UK Government 2.1–2.4 and 4.2	The ways in which parliament interacts with the executive
		Parliament and the executive
AQA	3.1.1.2 and 3.1.1.3	Scrutiny of the executive and the interaction of parliament with other branches of government

Context

While the power-balance between prime minister and parliament is invariably a delicate one, Boris Johnson's relationship with parliament is widely seen as one of the most complex and controversial of recent times. Over the course of his tenure in Number 10, the former prime minister stood accused of many things. His disruption to the parliamentary timetable through an unusually long prorogation (temporary discontinuation) was overturned by the Supreme Court and his bypassing parliament by making major policy announcements through the media was roundly condemned. Yet it was his misleading of parliament and his dismissiveness of parliamentary rules and customs that were to prove his eventual undoing.

A recent investigation by *The Independent* and the fact-checking organisation Full Fact established that Boris Johnson and his government made at least 27 false statements to parliament between 2019 and 2022, 17 of which came from the prime minister himself. The ministerial code is clear about the 'paramount importance' of truthfulness and accuracy and that any minister — including the prime minister — must correct any error 'at the earliest opportunity' but many of the false statements were never corrected.

As the misrepresentations increased, the relationship between executive and legislature worsened. The ambiguous statements made by Boris Johnson in parliament about his attendance at parties during lockdown were to provide the catalyst for a vote of no confidence that in turn led to a serious confrontation with the powerful House of Commons Liaison Committee. Despite a healthy election majority and robust levels of popularity among Conservative Party members, it was his parliamentary colleagues that were to put an end to Boris Johnson's premiership.

Three events in Boris Johnson's final months as prime minister helped to reshape parliament–executive relations:

- the extent to which Boris Johnson misled parliament over his attendance at social gatherings during lockdown
- the extent to which the parliamentary vote of no confidence in Boris Johnson irrecoverably damaged his leadership
- the effectiveness of the Liaison Committee in exposing the weakness of Boris Johnson's position, making his resignation all but inevitable.

Box 6.1   **'A fractious period for parliament'**

In an article in *The Conversation*, Louise Thompson, senior lecturer in Politics at the University of Manchester, commented that Boris Johnson's tenure exposed some of the most serious weaknesses in the functioning of the British constitution. The latter part of Boris Johnson's period as British prime minister characterised 'a fractious period for parliament and the wider political system' which had 'exposed some of the vulnerabilities of British constitutional norms'. Thompson pointed out how the blend of 'a strong parliamentary majority, ambiguous ministerial and parliamentary rules and a national crisis' can give prime ministers with a particularly strong power base the ability to 'dominate political life and avoid scrutiny'.

Source: 'Boris Johnson: four ways this controversial prime minister tested the British parliament to its limits, Louise Thompson, *The Conversation*, 2 September 2022 (https://theconversation.com)

What was the effect of Boris Johnson's misleading of parliament?

One of the most scrutinised periods of Boris Johnson's tenure came in early 2022 when the subject of social gatherings in defiance of lockdown regulations refused to leave the headlines. In early December 2021, during Prime Minister's Questions, Boris Johnson had repeatedly denied any wrongdoing. When Keir Starmer reminded the prime minister at the dispatch box that the rules clearly stated 'you must not have a work Christmas lunch or party', the prime minister responded by saying that 'all guidance was followed completely'.

Box 6.2 **What was parliament told about the lockdown parties?**

Accusations of unlawful parties in Downing Street were initially raised in parliament by opposition leader Keir Starmer at Prime Minister's Questions in early December 2021. Starmer asked 'as millions of people were locked down last year, was a Christmas party thrown in Downing Street for dozens of people on 18 December [2020]?'

Boris Johnson replied that 'all guidance was followed completely in Number 10'. To some people, it appeared that Boris Johnson was being vague about 'whether he meant all guidance was followed at all times during the pandemic, or whether he was specifically claiming that all guidance was followed on 18 December'.

However, just a few days later a video of the prime minister's Downing Street staff members was widely circulated. It showed them joking about whether there had been a Christmas party in Number 10. In parliament, Boris Johnson said that 'I have been repeatedly assured since these allegations emerged that there was no party and that no Covid rules were broken'. Later on the same day he told a Downing Street press conference that 'all the evidence I can see is that people in this building have stayed within the rules'.

Source: www.fullfact.org/news/partygate-parliament/

Six months later evidence emerged that Johnson had misled parliament. Alongside the publication of the report by Sue Gray into 'Partygate', came four images published by ITV News showing Boris Johnson in attendance at a gathering during the UK's second national lockdown in November 2020. These illustrative revelations backed up Sue Gray's report which stated clearly that the gatherings 'should not have been allowed to happen' and that since 'junior civil servants believed that their involvement in some of these events was permitted given the attendance of senior leaders... senior leadership at the centre, both political and official, must bear responsibility for this culture'. This appeared to fatally undermine Boris Johnson's assertions.

Box 6.3 **Sue Gray on the breach of Covid regulations**

Whatever the initial intent, what took place at many of these gatherings and the way in which they developed was not in line with Covid guidance at the time. Even allowing for the extraordinary pressures officials and advisers were under, the factual findings of this report illustrate some attitudes and behaviours inconsistent with that guidance. It is also clear, from the outcome of the police investigation, that the large number of individuals (83) who attended these events breached Covid regulations and therefore Covid guidance.

Source: report by senior civil servant Sue Gray 'Findings of the Second Permanent Secretary's Investigation into alleged gatherings on government premises during Covid restrictions', 25 May 2022

It was revealed in Sue Gray's report that Boris Johnson had attended nine of the 16 events that were investigated, though his attendance was brief at several. He had been issued with a Fixed Penalty Notice (FPN) for attending a party on 19 June 2020 as part of an investigation by the Metropolitan Police. The main allegation shifted to focus on whether he had intentionally misled parliament over the events of 13 November 2020. In this instance, the mismatch between what Boris Johnson said to parliament, and what the investigation report revealed, is stark.

Box 6.4 What happened on 13 November?

Sue Gray's report stated that Boris Johnson 'went to the Press Office area, joined the gathering and made a leaving speech for Lee Cain. Wine had been provided and those attending, including the Prime Minister, were drinking alcohol.'

What Boris Johnson said:

- On 8 December 2021 in parliament Catherine West, a Labour MP, asked: 'Will the Prime Minister tell the House whether there was a party in Downing Street on 13 November?' Boris Johnson responded: 'No, but I am sure that whatever happened, the guidance was followed and the rules were followed at all times.'
- On 19 April 2022 Boris Johnson made a statement to parliament saying that 'it did not occur to me, then or subsequently, that a gathering in the Cabinet Room just before a vital meeting on Covid strategy could amount to a breach of the rules. I repeat: that was my mistake and I apologise for it unreservedly.'
- On 25 May 2022 and in response to the publication of Sue Gray's report, Boris Johnson said in a statement to parliament that 'I came to this House and said in all sincerity that the rules and guidance had been followed at all times, it was what I believed to be true. It was certainly the case when I was present at gatherings to wish staff farewell, and my attendance at these moments, brief as it was, has not been found to be outside the rules.'

While Boris Johnson accepted that he had misled parliament, his statement in May indicated that he had done so inadvertently rather than knowingly. However, the breach was considered sufficiently serious to be referred for investigation by the cross-party Commons Privileges Committee, the findings of which would be voted on by parliament — a prospect which loomed large over the prime minister during the summer of 2022. With MPs on both sides of the chamber clearly understanding that the misleading of parliament represented a very serious matter, many of them found it increasingly difficult to reconcile what had been said previously by the prime minister with the subsequent findings of the investigation into the Downing Street parties.

What was the impact of the vote of confidence in Boris Johnson's leadership?

Within a fortnight of the publications of Sue Gray's report in early June 2022, the prime minister was said by many commentators to be 'clinging to his premiership' after 148 of his own MPs voted against him in a vote of confidence. The vote had been triggered after the threshold of 54 Conservative MPs had submitted letters of no confidence in the prime minister to the 1922 Committee.

While Johnson won the support of 211 of his own MPs, it was revealed in the clearest terms that 41% of his MPs did not have confidence in his leadership — the worst verdict on a sitting prime minister by their own party in recent times.

Comparisons between Boris Johnson's performance were immediately made with those of other recent prime ministers who had faced a similar vote as shown in Table 6.1.

Table 6.1 How damaging was the vote of confidence?

Year	Prime minister	% support of MPs	Effect
2022	Boris Johnson	59	Resigned within a month
2019	Theresa May	63	Resigned within 6 months
2003	Iain Duncan Smith	45	Lost the 2005 general election and resigned
1995	John Major	66	Lost the 1997 general election and resigned
1990	Margaret Thatcher	84	Resigned within a week

148 votes against Boris Johnson meant that the prime minister had effectively lost his majority support in parliament. Under Conservative Party rules, the prime minister was theoretically safe from another leadership challenge for 12 months but many pointed to the fact that Theresa May was forced to resign within 6 months of winning her confidence vote, having been terminally damaged despite a greater winning margin (200 votes to 117) than Boris Johnson had achieved.

While Boris Johnson claimed that it was an 'extremely good, positive, conclusive, decisive result' that enabled him to 'move on to unite and focus on delivery', the focus lay squarely on the fact that the proportion of his own MPs against him was larger than those against Theresa May in 2019 and Margaret Thatcher in 1990, both of whom resigned soon after, and the conclusion was that Boris Johnson's leadership was irrecoverably damaged.

The Commons Liaison Committee — the final blow

On 6 July 2022 the UK's prime minister faced the formidable prospect of a scheduled meeting with an empowered Liaison Committee at an extraordinarily challenging time for him. On the previous day Johnson's chancellor and health secretary had resigned after losing faith in the prime minister's leadership. A succession of other ministerial and government resignations followed, some of them occurring while the prime minister was responding to questions from the committee itself.

Box 6.5   What is the Commons Liaison Committee?

Since its inception in 2002, the Commons Liaison Committee has developed a growing reputation for shining the spotlight on the activities and performance of the prime minister, the government and the work of all the other Commons Select Committees. It comprises the chairpersons of the 33 House of Commons Select Committees and a chair.

A changed approach taken by the Liaison Committee has been instrumental in its evolved influence. In its infancy, committee members would customarily focus on questions generated by their own committees. Latterly however, the committee has found its own voice and has established a greater focus on single themes for each meeting. The impact of this focus can be substantial and invariably newsworthy.

- The Liaison Committee's relentless focus on Brexit during Theresa May's administration highlighted governing weakness and a lack of clear leadership.
- The Liaison Committee's scrutiny of Boris Johnson's personal conduct as well as of his government's handling of the Covid-19 health crisis contributed to his downfall.

The Liaison Committee focused unremittingly on Johnson's suitability to be prime minister. Front and centre were the integrity and personal ethics of the prime minister himself. Johnson's attendance at Downing Street gatherings in breach of lockdown rules and his handling of the conduct of the deputy chief whip, Chris Pincher, who had recently resigned following allegations of sexual assault, were contributory elements in an unremitting attack on his leadership qualities.

Box 6.6   Oblivious to the collapse of his government

In July 2022, Freddie Hayward wrote in the *New Statesman* that 'Boris Johnson sat before parliament's Liaison Committee earlier today clueless that his government was collapsing around him'. The challenges that were forthcoming 'from this crack squad of senior MPs descended into farce as it became clear that the man sat in the chair would soon no longer be prime minister'. While he was taking questions from the Liaison Committee, 'his cabinet colleagues were plotting to defenestrate him when he returned to Downing Street'.

Source: 'Boris Johnson's Liaison Committee appearance was a fittingly humiliating finale', Freddie Hayward, *The New Statesman*, 6 July 2022

Boris Johnson's 'exasperated and bullish' (according to *The New Statesman*) performance in front of the Liaison Committee led one opposition MP and committee member — the SNP's Angus Brendan MacNeil — to demand: 'the game's up — will you be prime minister tomorrow?' For many commentators, the performance left the prime minister beleaguered and isolated as the committee had amplified his leadership weaknesses. The prime minister insisted before the committee that he would 'not go anywhere', but his resignation came within 24 hours.

Exam success

The effectiveness of parliament in holding the executive to account is a central feature of the A-level politics course. The balance of power between the two branches of government is constantly changing and Boris Johnson's tenure in Number 10 and his relationship with parliament have added new dimensions to it. Essay questions in which recent events will feature prominently may be framed as follows:

- *Evaluate the extent to which parliament is no longer effective in holding the executive to account.* (Edexcel-style, 30 marks)
- *'Parliament is ineffective in holding the executive to account.' Analyse and evaluate this statement.* (AQA-style, 25 marks)

Recent parliamentary activity hastening the demise of Boris Johnson is a central element to high-level responses. These would need to be balanced against longer-term, structural factors such as the UK constitution's lack of codification to clearly frame the powers of both branches, the lack of separation of powers, which permits the executive to dominate the legislature, and a majoritarian electoral system, which routinely hands prime ministers over-large majorities.

That said, there is little doubt that the reassertion of parliament in the early 2020s and its central role in exposing the weaknesses in Boris Johnson's leadership has shifted analysis in this area. The reaction of MPs to undisputable evidence that the prime minister had misled the House, the momentum provided by governing-party MPs willing to vote against the leadership of a prime minister with a large majority, and the emboldening of the Commons Liaison Committee to become instrumental in the prime minister's demise are all thought-provoking and significant additions to the debate.

What next?

Watch: Prime Minister Boris Johnson giving evidence to the House of Commons Liaison Committee, 6 July 2022 (www.youtube.com/watch?v=zopEUw7gUMg).

Read: the 'Findings of the Second Permanent Secretary's Investigation into alleged gatherings on government premises during Covid restrictions' (www.gov.uk).

Chapter 7

Prime minister and executive (1): the rise and fall of Boris Johnson

Focus

Prime ministerial power and the relationships within the executive are prominent features of all examination specifications. Students are required to study the influence of at least two prime ministers, one from the period between 1945 and 1997 and one from the post-1997 period, to illustrate the effectiveness of prime ministers in dictating events and determining policy.

The Conservative Party won four successive general elections between 2010 and 2019, yet all election-winning prime ministers subsequently resigned — three in a period spanning just 6 years. The circumstances around the downfall of Boris Johnson provide further insight into the nature and scope of prime ministerial power. These events also provide evidence and examples of the checks on prime ministerial power, and the constraints exercised by a combination of cabinet colleagues, party, parliament and people.

Edexcel	UK Government 3.3	The prime minister and cabinet
AQA	3.1.1.3	Prime ministerial and cabinet power in dictating events and determining policy

Context

Boris Johnson fell from being golden boy of the Tory Party membership to parliamentary outsider in the space of just 3 years. While many former prime ministers have experienced a similar trajectory, few have travelled it so rapidly and so spectacularly.

To his supporters, Johnson will likely forever remain the celebrated maverick with the Midas touch, rising unstoppably for more than two decades from one high-profile political role to the next. In the eyes of his followers and in spite of all else, Johnson's delivery of both Brexit and a resounding Tory Party majority in the 2019 general election sets him apart from the many leaders who promise much but fail to deliver.

To illustrate his enduring appeal, in YouGov polls of Conservative Party members, conducted in August 2022, a majority of members still felt that it was wrong for MPs to have forced the resignation of Boris Johnson. Indeed, more members (40%) thought Johnson would make a better prime minister — even in spite of his recent resignation — than either of the then contenders, Liz Truss (28%) and Rishi Sunak (23%).

To his detractors, Johnson will live on as the prime minister whose personal qualities made him 'unfit for office' at the outset. Critics point to a tenure characterised by law breaking in office, a readiness to disregard rules that other people were bound by, and the repeated misrepresentation of events to parliament.

It would be fair to say that Boris Johnson was an intensely polarising figure. Whereas David Cameron had been consensus building, navigating 5 full years of coalition government, Boris Johnson's premiership was often seen through the lenses of division and conflict. Some of his closest fellow politicians, such as David Cameron and Michael Gove, became his most intense adversaries; some of his most trusted advisors, such Dominic Cummings and Munira Mirza, went on to become his most outspoken critics.

For students of politics, the most important considerations and questions relate to how and why Boris Johnson lost control, and how his demise provides further evidence of the changing relationships within the executive.

Box 7.1   Boris Johnson — the 'greased piglet'

Coined by David Cameron at the start of Boris Johnson's tenure in Number 10, the 'greased piglet' epithet was picked up by domestic and international media, political opponents and academics alike.

While Boris Johnson had himself used the term to describe past prime ministers, Cameron's likening of Johnson to a 'greased piglet' who 'manages to slip through other people's hands where mere mortals fail' seemed to characterise the new prime minister's supreme skill in 'getting away with it'.

In November 2019, *The Economist* elaborated on the 'four faces' of the UK's then new prime minister. As 'player, gambler, Machiavelli or piglet', Johnson's ability to 'either wriggle through loopholes or else shift the blame expertly to anyone but himself' was well-known prior to his accession to Number 10.

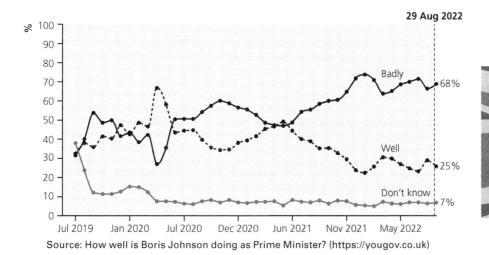

Source: How well is Boris Johnson doing as Prime Minister? (https://yougov.co.uk)

Figure 7.1 The rise and fall of Boris Johnson

The rise of Boris Johnson: from London Mayor to May's nemesis

Against seemingly insurmountable odds, Boris Johnson won the race to become the first Conservative Mayor of London in 2008. The capital city that regularly delivers more than double the number of Labour MPs to Conservative MPs proceeded to re-elect Johnson for a second term in 2012 during which time he was widely credited with delivering an Olympic games to global acclaim.

On leaving mayoral office, Johnson's backing of the Leave campaign in the Brexit referendum of 2016 is regarded as being pivotal to its success, lending credibility, charisma and appeal to what had seemed a lost cause with some previous opinion polls suggesting 'Remain' would secure the win. Johnson's canny withdrawal from the 2016 leadership race to replace David Cameron saw him elevated to cabinet status as foreign secretary under Theresa May, thereby providing him with the platform to unsettle her with a dramatic resignation. With no scars from a previous failed leadership bid, Johnson headed off Jeremy Hunt and became UK prime minister in the summer of 2019.

The fall of Boris Johnson: from prime minister to backbencher

While Theresa May's confirmatory general election in 2017 had proved disastrous, wiping out the hard-won Conservative Party majority of 2015, Johnson delivered an astonishing election win just over 2 years later, securing the biggest parliamentary majority for nearly 20 years, and the biggest Conservative party majority since the 1980s. His pledge to 'get Brexit done' tapped into the mood of frustrated voters from right across the political spectrum, leading to many formerly steadfast Labour Party constituencies 'turning blue' and returning a Conservative MP for the first time in over a century.

Johnson's handling of the Covid crisis was initially lauded as statesmanlike, his popularity as prime minister peaking in April 2020 when the crisis hit, and at the time of his admission to intensive care. Yet that was to be his high water mark. Despite a rally in popular support in the first half of 2021, from the spring of 2021 his demise was relentless. Amid repeated criticism of the government's response to the health crisis, personal accusations of unethical conduct, and allegations that he had lied to parliament, a catalogue of ministerial resignations in early July 2022 proved to be the end.

While it is difficult to pinpoint the precise 'beginning of the end' for Boris Johnson, the spring of 2021 saw the start of what became an irreversible decline in his popularity along with intense criticism of his personal and professional conduct (see Table 7.1).

Table 7.1 Notable events in Boris Johnson's demise, May 2021–July 2022

Date	Issue/Event	Details
May 2021	'Unfit to govern'	In nearly 7 hours of testimony to parliament, Johnson's former chief advisor Dominic Cummings accused Johnson of being 'unfit to govern'. According to Cummings, Johnson's disastrous handling of the pandemic had meant that 'tens of thousands of people died who didn't need to die'.
November 2021	Ethics reform u-turn	The Johnson government ordered its Conservative MPs to back an amendment to parliamentary ethics rules in support of Conservative MP Owen Paterson, who had been found guilty of breaching lobbying rules. In an embarrassing reversal, within 24 hours, the order was revoked and Owen Paterson resigned.
December 2021	'Partygate'	In the winter of 2021, rumours of Downing Street gatherings in breach of Covid-19 rules began to circulate. Johnson repeatedly denied all allegations of wrongdoing but speculation grew.
February 2022	Top aides quit	Munira Mirza, one of the prime minister's most trusted Downing Street advisors, quit, citing the false accusations that Johnson made in the House of Commons against Labour leader Keir Starmer, accusing him of failing to prosecute the paedophile Jimmy Savile. Other top aides quit too.
March 2022	Out of touch	As energy, fuel and food prices rose, Boris Johnson's government was criticised for not doing enough to support people struggling to cope. The government's mid-year spending plan was widely condemned as being out of touch.
April 2022	Law breaking	Johnson became the first UK prime minister to be found guilty of breaking the law while in office. Johnson admits breaching Covid-19 rules when attending a social event in 2021. The prime minister, along with other Downing Street party-goers, was fined £50.

Date	Issue/Event	Details
May 2022	Partygate report	Sue Gray's 'extremely critical' Partygate investigation report was published. The 60-page report covered 16 different events that had taken place on 12 different dates between May 2020 and April 2021. It cited a 'drinking culture' at the heart of government.
6 June 2022	No confidence vote	Johnson won a vote of no confidence despite an 'unexpectedly large' rebellion among Tory backbenchers. With 148 votes against him, the *Guardian* reported that he was 'clinging' to his premiership after the 'worst verdict on a sitting prime minister by their own party in recent times'.
15 June 2022	Resignation of ethics chief	Within a week of the no confidence vote, Johnson's ethics advisor Christopher (Lord) Geidt resigned over whether the prime minister had broken the ministerial code. It was the second resignation from an ethics advisor in less than 2 years.
30 June 2022	Support for Chris Pincher	Chris Pincher resigned as Conservative deputy chief whip amid allegations of sexual misconduct. As allegations of previous sexual misconduct emerged, questions were raised about whether Johnson knew about this when Chris Pincher got the job.
5–6 July 2022	Ministerial resignations	Johnson apologised for promoting Chris Pincher but many senior cabinet ministers, including Chancellor Rishi Sunak and Health Secretary Sajid Javid, resigned. Over 30 senior and junior ministers resigned over Johnson's conduct and leadership.
7 July 2022	Resignation	Boris Johnson resigned as Conservative Party leader and British prime minister.

How and why did Boris Johnson 'lose control'?

While numerous prime ministers are the victims of events often outside of their immediate control, for many, Boris Johnson appeared to be the architect of his own downfall in several instances. That said, for a relentlessly 'feel good' prime minister, reliant on 'boosterism' — deflecting criticism through relentless enthusiasm and confidence — the health crisis was a disaster. Yet there are several specific and notable events and issues in the 12 months leading up to his resignation that combined to force the prime minister's hand.

Factor 1: Owen Paterson and 'a total mistake'

In October 2021, a 2-year investigation into Owen Paterson's paid advocacy reported that he had 'repeatedly used his privileged position to benefit two companies for whom he was a paid consultant, and that this has brought the House into disrepute'. The Commons Select Committee on Standards reviewed the investigation by the Parliamentary Commissioner for Standards and recommended that Owen Paterson be suspended from the House of Commons for 30 days.

With Owen Paterson furiously criticising the investigatory process and its verdict as defying 'natural justice', many Conservative MPs rallied in support. The government sought to block the judgement by seeking to rewrite the standards system. Conservative whips demanded that MPs support an amendment to this effect, which passed by 250 votes to 232. Accusations of sleaze followed as the manipulation of the system in favour of a colleague stuck to the front pages. Within 24 hours, Boris Johnson withdrew his support, leaving many Conservative MPs embarrassed and disappointed by his leadership.

Box 7.2   A 'total mistake'

I think it was a total mistake not to see that the former member for North Shropshire's breach of the rules made any discussion about anything else impossible. And I totally accept that. I think it was a very sad case, but I think there's no question that he had fallen foul of the rules on paid advocacy, as far as I could see from the report.

Source: Boris Johnson's responses to the Commons Liaison Committee, November 2021

Factor 2: Partygate and 'falling short'

In the spring and summer of 2022 the Metropolitan Police issued 126 fines to 83 people for breaches of Covid regulations at Downing Street and Whitehall. Boris Johnson apologised for attending a number of social events in and around Downing Street and accepted a £50 fine for attending a gathering on his birthday in June 2020.

Media reports and widespread speculation prompted the launch of an internal investigation into the nature and purpose of the Downing Street gatherings in potential breach of Covid rules. Sue Gray, a senior civil servant, was tasked with leading the investigation. She was especially critical in her May 2022 report of the behaviour, leadership and lack of respect for and poor treatment of security and cleaning staff that pervaded Downing Street.

Box 7.3   An 'unacceptable' lack of respect

What took place at many of these gatherings and the way in which they developed was not in line with Covid guidance at the time... The public have a right to expect the very highest standards of behaviour in such places, and clearly what happened fell well short of this. [Some staff had] witnessed or been subjected to behaviours at work which they had felt concerned about but at times felt unable to raise properly.

Source: Sue Gray's investigation into Downing Street parties, May 2022

Factor 3: Chris Pincher and 'no excuse'

A week before Boris Johnson's resignation allegations emerged about the behaviour of the Conservative deputy chief whip Chris Pincher. On 30 June 2022 the deputy chief whip admitted 'embarrassing himself' by drinking too much and assaulting other members at a London club the previous evening. Further allegations about the deputy chief whip's previous behaviour followed.

Downing Street claimed that Boris Johnson was not aware of allegations of misbehaviour about Chris Pincher, a line supported by ministers for several days. However by 4 July Lord McDonald, a former civil servant, revealed that Boris Johnson's denial was 'not true', and that he was told in person of a formal complaint back in 2019, yet still appointed Chris Pincher as deputy chief whip.

Box 7.4 **'I should have acted on it'**

There was one complaint that was raised with me specifically… it was a long time ago and it was raised orally with me… but that is no excuse, I should have acted on it.

Source: Boris Johnson in a BBC interview on 5 July 2022

Factor 4: Policy and ideas — a 'shopping trolley'

While factors well beyond Boris Johnson's control contributed to some of the most difficult economic issues as the world emerged from Covid, specific government policies were widely condemned as being 'out of touch'. Against a backdrop of sharply rising inflation and record energy prices, Keir Starmer criticised the April 2022 rise in National Insurance, demanding to know why 'the government chooses to increase taxes on working people' amid 'the worst cost of living crisis for decades'.

To many critics, when the sharp focus on getting Brexit done that won Boris Johnson his resounding majority in 2019 had dissipated, there appeared to be no coherent policies to move on to. His former advisor Dominic Cummings had previously likened him to 'an out-of-control shopping trolley', devoid of clear principles and policies. It was a caricature that stuck. His former Conservative Party leadership opponent Jeremy Hunt echoed many when he accused Boris Johnson in the summer of 2022 of lacking 'integrity, competence and vision'.

Box 7.5 **'Just like a shopping trolley'**

Everybody was screaming on quarantine 'have a policy and set it out clearly and stick to it'. We cannot keep changing our mind every time the *Telegraph* writes an editorial on the subject. Everybody agreed with me about that, regardless of what they thought the real policy should be. No one could find a way around the problem of the Prime Minister [being] just like a shopping trolley smashing from one side of the aisle to the other.

Source: former Number 10 aide, Dominic Cummings, at a marathon joint session of parliament's health and science committees, May 2021

There was to be one short-lived and surprising return to the limelight for Boris Johnson. As the Conservative Party reeled following the extraordinarily rapid departure of Prime Minister Liz Truss in October 2022, the former Downing Street incumbent, returning from holiday in the Dominican Republic, briefly declared himself 'up for it' before pulling out of the contest the day before nominations were due to be declared (see chapter 9). Boris Johnson's claim that he would have secured the required 100 pledged MPs in support of his nomination is set to remain unverified.

Box 7.6 'Not the right time'

Sky News's political editor Beth Rigby charted Boris Johnson's 'mad dash' back from his Caribbean holiday in late October to engage in 'a flurry of canvassing, secret summits with rivals Rishi Sunak and Penny Mordaunt'. Despite the public backing of a number of prominent MPs, the former prime minister announced that he wouldn't be standing after all.

Rigby commented that it 'was the most Boris Johnson way of admitting defeat'. She quoted him as saying 'I... could deliver a Conservative victory in 2024, I have the numbers' (he claimed 102 supporters) but that 'now is not the time'.

Source: Beth Rigby quoted in *Sky News* article 'Not the right time': Johnson pulls out of leadership race, 24 October 2022.

Ultimately, mistakes and complaints coalesced into an irresistible wave of opposition within his own ranks leaving him out of control of day-to-day events in cabinet and parliament. Less than 3 years after leading the Conservatives to their biggest election win in nearly 40 years, Boris Johnson lost the support of his party in the House of Commons and resigned.

Exam success

Boris Johnson's tenure in Number 10 and the manner of his departure provide good material for essays on the nature and scope of prime ministerial power and the relationships within the executive. Essay questions may focus on the balance between cabinet and prime ministerial government. For example:

- *Evaluate the view that the powers of the prime minister are outweighed by the constraints of the cabinet.* (Edexcel-style, 30 marks)
- *'Prime ministers dominate their cabinets.' Analyse and evaluate this statement.* (AQA-style, 25-marks)

Responses may include the following points. For each of them, there is a suitable example from Boris Johnson's term in office.

Table 7.2 Prime ministerial powers and constraints

Factor	Power	Constraint
Theories of prime ministerial predominance	There is little doubt that the PM dominates UK politics, making all the major decisions. The position has long since outgrown its 'first among equals' origins.	The PM needs the support of his/her cabinet to survive. While cabinet colleagues are likely to be the staunchest supporters, their backing cannot be taken for granted.
Patronage powers and expectations of loyalty	Most cabinet members owe their appointments and continued ministerial roles to the incumbent PM. Their cabinet positions come with expectations of loyalty.	The most effective cabinets are drawn from all elements of the party. An imbalanced 'sycophantic' cabinet will alienate the parliamentary party while a 'balanced' cabinet will check the PM's power.
Cabinet management	PMs control the agenda and timing of cabinet meetings. Contentious topics are sometimes sidelined or decided in committees away from the main cabinet. Full cabinet meetings can often lack meaningful debate.	Cabinet dissatisfaction and ultimately resignations can be particularly hazardous for the PM. Many prime ministers may have lost the support of their party, parliament and people. But when senior cabinet figures desert them, their time is up.
Events and circumstances	Large parliamentary majorities, prominence in world events, favourable media coverage, stable economic growth all conspire to make many a PM seem almost invincible. Cabinets can have little influence or power.	Small majorities, economic difficulties or difficult domestic and global events can ensure that PMs have greater reliance on their cabinets. Good cabinets can become effective, collective decision-making bodies when they are most needed.
The PM's Office	The growth in the PM's and Cabinet Office has provided the PM with a powerful personal bureaucracy, allowing him/her to take on large governmental matters and drive through personal policy with a skilled and loyal team.	Despite its recent growth, the office of the UK's political head of state is substantially smaller than the resources available to the US president.

What next?

Watch: 'The rise and fall of Boris Johnson', a *Newsnight* film presented by Michael Cockerell, 5 September 2022 (www.bbc.com).

Read:

- 'Boris Johnson didn't want to quit. So how did they get rid of him?', a commentary on Boris Johnson's resignation, *The Washington Post*, 8 July 2022 (www.washingtonpost.com).
- Sue Gray's full report into the Downing Street parties 'Findings of the Second Permanent Secretary's Investigation into alleged gatherings on government premises during Covid restrictions' (www.gov.uk).

Chapter 8

Prime minister and executive (2): Liz Truss — how and why did it all go so wrong?

Focus

Students need a thorough knowledge of all aspects of the UK's executive and its relationship with other branches of government. The topic also encompasses the roles and responsibilities, powers and constraints of the prime minister and his/her relationship with cabinet colleagues as well as the factors at play when considering the prime minister's selection of cabinet colleagues.

Edexcel	UK Government 3.2 and 3.3	The factors that affect the relationship between the cabinet and prime minister
AQA	3.1.1.3	The relationship between the prime minister and cabinet

Context

On 6 September 2022 Liz Truss travelled to Balmoral in Scotland for an appointment with the queen. According to established convention, as leader of the largest party in the House of Commons, she was invited by the monarch to become prime minister of Great Britain and Northern Ireland and asked to form a government on behalf of the Crown.

Later that day, and in her first address as prime minister, Downing Street's newest incumbent declared that with her 'hands on' style of government, the UK would 'ride out the storm' of the cost of living crisis with plans to cap spiralling energy bills.

Yet in an extraordinary turn of events, under 7 weeks later Liz Truss was again standing in front of the door of Number 10 making her final address as prime minister after a calamitous mini-budget, the resignation of prominent ministers and an irredeemable loss of confidence among almost all Conservative MPs.

The resignation meant that while the UK had had just four prime ministers spanning over three decades between 1979 and 2010, the resignation of the fourth Conservative Party prime minister in a little over 6 years had paved the way, within just 2 months, for the fifth. David Cameron and Theresa May were both casualties of Brexit, Boris Johnson and Liz Truss could not command the trust and confidence of their cabinet colleagues or parliamentary parties. For many commentators, expectations, events and the demands and complexities of the office appear to have proved increasingly difficult to manage.

Table 8.1 Conservative prime ministers' resignations 2010–22

Dates	Prime minister	Reason for resigning
2010–16	David Cameron	Campaigned for the UK to remain in the EU and resigned following Leave victory in the 2016 referendum.
2016–19	Theresa May	Declared that 'Brexit means Brexit' but resigned after the party lost confidence in her administration's ability to deliver it.
2019–22	Boris Johnson	Secured the largest government majority since 2001, got Brexit 'done' but lost the trust of cabinet colleagues after successive scandals.
2022 (September) – 2022 (October)	Liz Truss	After an unfunded mini-budget and a mishandling of a confidence vote, Truss declared that she could not 'deliver the mandate on which I was elected by the Conservative party'.

Despite the brevity of Liz Truss's tenure, understanding her background and elevation, analysing her election as party leader, the basis for the appointment of her cabinet colleagues and assessing the factors surrounding her rapid demise are integral parts of essays evaluating the power and responsibilities of the prime minister.

Truss the ambitious pragmatist

The MP for South West Norfolk has had a comparatively rapid rise to Number 10 following her election to parliament in 2010. Liz Truss's first cabinet position was as environment secretary in David Cameron's government in 2014. She went on to serve under Cameron as justice secretary, then under Theresa May as chief secretary to the Treasury. Appointments as international trade secretary and most recently foreign secretary under Boris Johnson followed.

As the likelihood of her winning the party leadership grew in 2022, so too did a wider exploration of her track record. While it would be fair to say that many senior politicians travel wide-ranging ideological journeys to reach their political 'enlightenment', the incoming prime minister's former Liberal Democrat activism, her marches against the Thatcher government's decision to allow US nuclear weapons into the UK, and her youthful protests against the monarchy did not stand in the way of her selection as Conservative Party leader.

Box 8.1 Liz Truss and her Liberal Democrat past: 'we all make mistakes'

Prior to securing the South West Norfolk seat ahead of the 2010 general election, Liz Truss had an edgy path towards a Conservative Party nomination. At an unsuccessful hustings in Eastbourne, she responded to some jeers from the audience by saying: 'We all make mistakes, we all had teenage misadventures, and that was mine. Some people have sex, drugs and rock and roll, I was in the Liberal Democrats. I'm sorry.'

Liz Truss and Brexit

The most notable reversal in Liz Truss's career came over Brexit. In the 2016 referendum she was an ardent supporter of Remain while serving in David Cameron's government. Since then, according to Rafael Behr in the *Guardian*, she has become one of the most 'zealous converts' to the Brexit cause.

In 2016 Liz Truss tweeted:

> I am backing remain as I believe it is in Britain's economic interest and means we can focus on vital economic and social reform at home.

and:

> Leave cannot name one country we would get a better trade deal with if we left the EU.

Yet on the BBC's *Daily Politics*, October 2017 she said:

> ... we've seen since the Brexit vote that our economy has done well... we haven't seen the dire predictions come to pass. We have seen new opportunities to trade with the rest of the world, I think that's exciting.

That said, Liz Truss appears to have acknowledged her change of heart over Brexit more readily than many. Since the 2016 referendum, she has emphasised her view that the vote to leave was as much about the EU as it was 'an expression about what kind of country we wanted to be'. And from 2019, she became instrumental in supporting Boris Johnson to 'get Brexit done'. As foreign secretary, Liz Truss called the EU 'protectionist' and said that the UK had 'lost [its] trade muscle memory... as a sovereign trading nation' but was 'building it back' since departing from the EU.

How did Liz Truss secure the party leadership?

Four days after Boris Johnson's resignation in July 2022, Liz Truss announced her intention to run for the leadership of the Conservative Party. Burnishing her conservative credentials, she pledged to 'fight the election as a Conservative and govern as a Conservative', focusing on tackling the cost of living crisis, scaling back the size of the state and reducing the tax burden on individuals and businesses.

The eight candidates who started the race were whittled down to two after successive votes by Conservative Party MPs and on 20 July 2022, Liz Truss (113 votes) and Rishi Sunak (137 votes) won through to the membership vote. Just over 170,000 registered Conservative Party members have played an extraordinarily prominent role in determining successive political heads of state for the UK in recent years, and it was to them again that the final decision fell.

Many commentators highlighted the significant difference in the two candidates over their support for Boris Johnson. While Rishi Sunak's resignation proved fatal for Johnson, Liz Truss had remained loyal — something that played decisively well with the many Johnson loyalists within the membership.

Table 8.2 Conservative Party leadership election — members' vote

Candidate	Votes	% of votes cast
Liz Truss	81,326	57.4
Rishi Sunak	60,339	42.6

Turnout among party members: 82.2%

For many, Liz Truss had long sought to cultivate a specifically Thatcher-like 'iron lady' image. Perhaps the biggest similarity between the two prime ministers on assuming office was the size of the challenge that awaited them. Inflation at a 40-year high, soaring energy bills, a declining pound, record borrowing and rising interest rates presented formidable difficulties for the incoming prime minister.

Yet unlike Thatcher, in seeing through her leadership election pledge to radically reposition the UK economy, driving economic growth with a tax-cutting agenda, Liz Truss proved herself unable to command the confidence of her own MPs.

Box 8.3 A 'gargantuan task'

Not only does she have one of the most troublesome in-trays that any incoming PM has had post-war, healing the wounds caused by a fierce leadership election and uniting her party at the same time is going to take some doing — especially given she may have to announce large pandemic-esque support packages to help Britons through the economic backdrop she's inheriting.

Source: Chris Hopkins, Director of Political Research at Savanta ComRes, 6 September 2022

What factors shaped the selection of Truss's cabinet?

The first appointments made by an incoming prime minister are often regarded as the easiest. On a wave of affirmation, optimism and strength, the new PM has the pick of his/her colleagues, with opportunities to reward loyal followers, forgive less than fulsome supporters, and gratifyingly sideline former colleagues who opposed or offended.

That said, the first appointments are subject to more intense scrutiny as likely to set the tone for the years to come. A firm feature of the prevailing advice for an incoming prime minister is caution not to fill senior positions purely on the basis of personal loyalty over experience and ability.

The arrival of a new PM is also accompanied by a raft of resignations from ministers within the former administration. Those accompanying Boris Johnson out of office included Home Secretary Priti Patel, Deputy Prime Minister Dominic Raab, Transport Secretary Grant Shapps, and Secretary of State for Digital, Culture, Media and Sport Nadine Dorries.

The 'big jobs' go to staunch supporters

Prime ministers have a natural disposition to reward those instrumental in their success, and to rely on trusted colleagues, particularly as they adjust to the expectations and challenges of the Downing Street role. That said, Peter Walker in the *Guardian* noted 'how uniformly the top of Truss's cabinet is a mix of friends, former colleagues and ideological soulmates. But most of all, supporters'.

The ideological soulmate

Kwasi Kwarteng, the chancellor of the exchequer, was elected as an MP in 2010, entering parliament at the same time as Liz Truss. He had 4 years of ministerial experience, most recently as business secretary during which time he clashed with Truss's eventual leadership opponent, Rishi Sunak. Kwarteng is widely regarded as sharing the same economic outlook as Truss and along with the new PM was a co-author of *Britannia Unchained*, a 2012 collection of essays advocating a small-state UK.

The apprentice

James Cleverly, the foreign secretary, spent 2 years as a junior minister working directly under Liz Truss in the foreign office. Critics of his appointment suggest that in elevating Cleverly, Truss allowed herself to retain a firm control of the department from Number 10, especially amid particularly turbulent global affairs. Cleverly was among the earliest backers of Liz Truss, and focused criticism on her rival, Rishi Sunak for being slow to respond to concerns about the influence of China.

The close friend

Appointed as a trusted 'second-in-command', Thérèse Coffey was referred to by *The Independent* as Liz Truss's 'long-time ally and fellow karaoke enthusiast'. Seen as Liz Truss's closest friend in Westminster, Coffey became both health secretary and deputy prime minister. Their friendship predates their appointment as MPs though they have both represented near-neighbouring eastern England constituencies since 2010.

Table 8.3 Senior cabinet figures appointed by Liz Truss — the top ten key roles

Role	Minister
Deputy prime minister and secretary of state for health and social care	Thérèse Coffey
Chancellor of the exchequer	Kwasi Kwarteng
Secretary of state for foreign, Commonwealth and development affairs	James Cleverly
Secretary of state for the home department	Suella Braverman
Secretary of state for justice and lord chancellor	Brandon Lewis
Chancellor of the Duchy of Lancaster and equalities minister	Nadhim Zahawi
Secretary of state for defence	Ben Wallace
Secretary of state for business, energy and industrial strategy	The Rt Hon. Jacob Rees-Mogg MP
Secretary of state for education	The Rt Hon. Kit Malthouse MP
Leader of the House of Commons	The Rt Hon. Penny Mordaunt MP

The exonerated former opponents

Former attorney general Suella Braverman was appointed as Liz Truss's first home secretary. Braverman stood against the new PM in the first round of the leadership contest, but her commitment to the right of the Conservative Party and her prior experience as a barrister and attorney general saw her recruited in a top role.

The day before Liz Truss herself resigned, Suella Braverman resigned with a scathing criticism of Truss's 'tumultuous' time in office after sending a confidential Home Office document using her personal email.

Penny Mordaunt failed to win through to the final round of the leadership contest but endorsed Liz Truss as the 'hope candidate' on her departure from it. Equally, the new PM saw in Penny Mordaunt a colleague who could shore up support in the parliamentary party, in which Truss's support was regarded as being shaky at best. Mordaunt was appointed as leader of the House of Commons.

A diverse cabinet?

Liz Truss was widely regarded as having selected the most diverse cabinet ever appointed in terms of gender and ethnicity. Liz Truss herself is only the third female to hold the office of prime minister, and both of the others (Margaret Thatcher and Theresa May) have been Conservative leaders too.

Box 8.5 **UK PM Liz Truss appoints diverse cabinet in shake-up of old guard**

According to *The Hindu Times*, Prime Minister Liz Truss unveiled one of the UK's most diverse cabinets, with key frontline posts going to ethnic minority members of parliament. By her side would be:

- Ghanian-origin Kwasi Kwarteng as the UK's first black chancellor
- Indian-origin Suella Braverman as home secretary, whose Tamil mother had her family roots in Mauritius and Goan-origin father migrated to the UK from Kenya.
- Mixed Sierra Leone and white heritage James Cleverly as the foreign secretary. Cleverly has spoken about being bullied as a mixed-race child and has said the party needs to do more to attract black voters.

Source: adapted from *The Hindu Times*, 7 September 2022

In addition, it was widely reported that the new PM had selected a cabinet where for the first time a white man did not hold one of the country's four most important ministerial positions. It would seem that the upper ranks of politics are benefitting from concerted drives, especially by the Conservative Party, to put forward a more varied set of candidates for parliament in recent years.

Where did it all go wrong?

The calamity of the mini-Budget in September 2022, which sent the main UK stockmarkets and the pound sharply falling, was to prove irreparable for Liz Truss. Her failure to explain how such radical decisions would be paid for was seen by many Conservatives as an irresponsible shredding of their party's reputation for fiscal responsibility. Sacking close ally Kwasi Kwarteng as chancellor after just 38 days in the job, replacing him with Jeremy Hunt who reversed the mini-Budget (along with the associated tax cuts upon which Truss was elected leader) stabilised little. A YouGov poll taken 2 days prior to Truss's resignation confirmed that 77% or respondents 'disapproved' of the Conservative government.

Truss's lack of public appearances during this period of instability convinced many that events were out of her control. Matters were hardly helped by Penny Mordaunt who, while standing in for Liz Truss in parliament, insisted that the prime minister was 'not under a desk' hiding. Rather than dispelling the image, it served to lodge it fixedly in the public consciousness.

The final nail in the Truss premiership came on 19 October, when chaos in the Westminster voting lobbies ensued as no one, including the Conservative whips, appeared to know whether a vote on a fracking ban had been declared a confidence motion in the government, in a miscalculated attempt to show strength.

U-turns on flagship economic policies and a complete loss of authority had confirmed to the large majority of Conservative MPs that Liz Truss was incapable of leading the party, government and country effectively.

> **Box 8.6** **Liz Truss: 'I am resigning as leader of the Conservative Party'**
>
> Liz Truss announced her resignation in a televised press conference outside Downing Street at 1.30 p.m. on Thursday 20 October. Speaking about her brief time in office, Truss claimed that her government 'had delivered on energy bills and on cutting national insurance' and 'set out a vision for a low-tax, high-growth economy that would take advantage of the freedoms of Brexit'.

What next?

Review: The Institute for Government's commentary on the cabinet appointments process, 'Liz Truss government formation – live blog' (www.instituteforgovernment.org.uk).

Read:

- The LSE blog 'What should the next UK prime minister do?', Anna Valero and John Van Reenen, 2 September 2020 (https://blogs.lse.ac.uk).
- 'Why Liz Truss resigned as UK prime minister: A guide to the chaos' by Leo Sands, Adela Suliman and Karla Adam, *The Washington Post*, October 20, 2022 (www.washingtonpost.com).

Chapter 9

Prime minister and executive (3): the early days of new Prime Minister Rishi Sunak

Focus

Examination specifications require students to understand the powers of the prime minister and to assess their strength relative to their cabinet and parliament. In order to evaluate the role of the prime minister thoroughly, students need to compare and contrast the methods and levels of success of different prime ministers. Being able to analyse the prime minister currently holding office is crucial is this fast-moving subject.

Edexcel	UK Government 3.3	The prime minister and cabinet
AQA	3.1.1.3	The prime minister and the cabinet

Context

The resignation of Liz Truss on 21 October 2022 triggered the second Conservative Party leadership contest of the year. Under the rules set out by the 1922 Committee of backbench Conservative MPs, any candidate wishing to stand was required to gain the backing of at least 100 of his/her fellow MPs. In the event that more than three candidates received the necessary backing, a vote of MPs would eliminate the least popular candidate. The remaining two candidates would then be voted on by the Conservative Party members, with their preferred choice being crowned leader of the Conservative Party.

Only three candidates expressed public interest in the leadership: Boris Johnson, Penny Mordaunt and Rishi Sunak. Johnson withdrew from the race the night before the vote, saying that although he had enough support from MPs to stand, it was 'not the right time'. Mordaunt, who did not have the necessary number of endorsements from Tory MPs, withdrew shortly before voting was due to take place. Sunak was, therefore, unopposed and was confirmed as the new Conservative Party leader on 24 October 2022, without a vote of either MPs or Conservative Party members. Sunak was formally appointed as prime minister the following day by King Charles III. He is Britain's first prime minister of Indian heritage.

What is Rishi Sunak's background?

Rishi Sunak is the son of a doctor and a pharmacist. He was privately educated at Winchester College, read Politics, Philosophy and Economics at Lincoln College, Oxford and then studied for an MBA at Stanford University in the United States.

He worked in investment banking and for hedge funds before being elected MP for Richmond in Yorkshire in 2015. Partly because of his own success in business and partly because of his wife's wealth (his wife, Akshata Murthy, is the daughter of Indian billionaire N. R. Narayana Murthy), Sunak is Britain's wealthiest member of parliament.

Sunak sat on the backbenches until 2018, when Theresa May appointed him parliamentary under-secretary of state for local government. Under Johnson, whose 2019 candidacy for leader of the Conservative Party he supported, Sunak was promoted first to chief secretary of the treasury and then to the post of chancellor of the exchequer. As chancellor, Sunak was responsible for the Coronavirus job retention scheme and the 'Eat Out to Help Out' initiative.

Sunak's relationship with Johnson had soured by mid-2022. A key cause of political disagreement was whether to impose a windfall tax on energy companies, a measure Johnson supported and Sunak opposed. Sunak had also become increasingly frustrated by Johnson's conduct as prime minister, saying in his resignation letter of 5 July that 'the public rightly expect government to be conducted properly, competently and seriously'. A wave of other ministers followed Sunak in resigning and his decision to step down is generally seen as triggering Johnson's downfall.

Sunak stood in the race to replace Johnson as Conservative Party leader but when offered a choice between him and Liz Truss, the Conservative Party membership preferred Truss. She won 57.4% of the vote to his 42.6%. Fortunately for Sunak her difficult period in office provided him with another chance at the top job.

Why did Conservative MPs choose Rishi Sunak?

Members of parliament had a variety of reasons for putting their trust in Sunak:

- As an early supporter of Brexit, Sunak is acceptable to those MPs who supported Britain's withdrawal from the European Union. Sunak is also seen as having the necessary experience to lead the country through its economic difficulties, having been chancellor of the exchequer during the Coronavirus crisis.
- Another point in Sunak's favour is that his attitude to policy making has always been pragmatic, rather than ideological. For example, he introduced the job retention scheme during the pandemic. This massively increased government spending and state involvement in the economy, two things Sunak would have preferred to avoid but recognised were necessary in the situation. This pragmatic approach to policy is seen by many in the Conservative parliamentary party as the best way to manage the economy over the coming months and years.
- Sunak has a reputation for treating other policy-making dilemmas in the same way. He listens to different perspectives and ideas, and examines the evidence before making decisions. This makes him very different from either Johnson or Truss. This change in style of leadership will, Conservative MPs hope, ensure

sound policy making. MPs also hope that it will appeal to the British public, who are, they fear, tired of a government that has often been portrayed in the media as chaotic.

■ Sunak benefitted too from opinion polls, which suggest he presents a strong challenge to an increasingly powerful Labour Party. In an Ipsos-Mori poll taken on the 19 and 20 October 2022, 36% of voters said they thought that Sunak would do a good job as PM. Starmer had more support, with 42% of those surveyed saying that they thought he would do a good job as PM but the gap between the two men is relatively narrow. Under Truss, the Conservative Party slumped to its lowest ever poll ratings, so regaining the support of the voters is vital for a party that wants to win the next election.

What are Sunak's priorities for the country?

In a speech given outside 10 Downing Street shortly after he took the reins of power, Sunak explained that his first priority would be to recreate 'economic stability and confidence'. He pledged to do this while offering as much protection as he could to people and businesses but cautioned that there were limits to what government could achieve. These limits would not, Sunak promised, prevent him making repayments on government debt. Indeed, he pledged that the children of today will not spend their adult lives paying off debts run up by Conservative governments.

As ambitious as his economic plans is Sunak's desire to 'unite the country' by leading an administration with 'professionalism, integrity and accountability' that will win people's trust. He intends to do this alongside fulfilling the policy aims of the 2019 manifesto, including a 'stronger NHS, better schools, safer streets, control of our borders, protecting our environment, supporting our armed forces, levelling up and building an economy that embraces the opportunities of Brexit'. Stressing his support for the 2019 manifesto is a way of emphasising the legitimacy of Sunak's government because it was on these manifesto promises that the party was elected. It also sets him apart from Truss, who claimed that her election by the Conservative Party membership gave her a mandate for policies not included in the 2019 manifesto.

Can Sunak restore unity to the Conservative Party?

Sunak will not be successful as leader of the Conservative Party unless he can restore the unity and order that were eroded under Johnson and completely lost during Truss's brief premiership. A number of decisions made by Johnson divided the Conservative parliamentary party. In October 2019 he removed the whip from 21 Conservative MPs who had voted with the opposition in the Commons in an attempt to prevent a no deal Brexit. Among those who had the whip removed from them were highly respected members of the party, such as Kenneth Clarke, who had served as chancellor of the exchequer under Margaret Thatcher, and Winston Churchill's grandson, Nicholas Soames. Johnson's decision to impose restrictions on public freedom in response to the Coronavirus pandemic also drew criticism from within his own party. In December 2021, 96 Conservative MPs voted against a government bill to mandate vaccine certificates for those wanting to visit public places. Johnson's behaviour also made him unpopular with his own MPs, with many angry that he had hosted parties at 10 Downing Street during lockdown.

Truss's unpopularity stemmed from creating a cabinet staffed almost entirely by her own supporters. By tradition, prime ministers include representatives from across the range of their party in their cabinets. Truss lost even more support when the financial markets reacted negatively to her mini-budget and she was forced to U-turn on most of its policies. Conservative MPs started to openly question her judgement and ability to do the job of prime minister. On 13 October, *The Times* published an article in which Conservative MP Robert Halfon accused Liz Truss of 'trashing the last 10 years', while Michael Gove described Truss's economic policies as 'profoundly concerning'.

Restoring unity to the Conservative Party will be a difficult job for Sunak. Different factions within the party have completely different priorities. The European Research Group would like lower taxes, less government spending and a smaller state, while the Northern Research Group of MPs want more government spending in deprived constituencies to fulfil the 2019 election manifesto promise of 'levelling up' (increasing the prosperity of poorer areas of the UK).

In the short term these factions within the Conservative Party will probably be prepared to keep a low profile because they realise that the more split the party appears the less appealing they are to the electorate. This should help Sunak but he cannot rely on the loyalty of all his MPs. For example, within 48 hours of Sunak becoming prime minister, Conservative MP Caroline Noakes questioned his judgement in appointing Suella Braverman as home secretary.

The way in which Sunak has assembled his first cabinet may also help keep the party on his side. Unlike Johnson or Truss, he has chosen figures from across the party to work in his government:

- Chancellor of the Exchequer Jeremy Hunt served as foreign secretary under Theresa May and stood against Johnson for the leadership of the Conservative Party in 2019. Hunt backed 'remain' at the time of the Brexit referendum.
- Suella Braverman was reappointed to the position of home secretary 6 days after resigning from the same position in Truss's cabinet, after admitting to breaching the ministerial code. Braverman has a lot of support from the pro-Brexit European Research Group within the Conservative Party.
- Foreign Secretary James Cleverly also retained the role he held under Liz Truss. Like Braverman he is a supporter of Brexit.
- Dominic Raab, who lost his cabinet position under Truss, found himself restored to the two posts he held under Johnson, deputy prime minister and justice secretary.

- Another member of the Johnson cabinet who returned to his previous job is Michael Gove, who found himself again fulfilling the role of levelling up secretary.

More junior cabinet posts were also distributed in a way that shows that Sunak is serious about representing all elements of the Conservative Party in his government:

- Andrew Mitchell and Tom Tugendhat, both severe critics of the Johnson administration, were appointed minister for development and minister for security respectively. Mitchell and Tugendhat are generally seen as being on the left of the Conservative Party.
- Secretary of State for International Trade Kemi Badenoch, on the other hand, is on the right of the party. She is socially conservative and has been very vocal in her criticism of what she characterises as 'woke' culture. She is opposed, for example, to gender neutral bathrooms and to allowing trans people to choose whether to identify as male or female in their workplaces.

The difficulty with assembling a broad-based cabinet will be keeping everyone on side. Unless he can maintain collective responsibility, Sunak will look weak. The experience of Johnson and Truss shows, however, that even if you only appoint those you see as loyal to your cabinet you can still struggle to get them to maintain consensus in public.

Rishi Sunak has taken over as prime minister at an extremely difficult time for the country and the Conservative Party. It will take time, careful policy making and excellent communication with both his MPs and the general public to achieve his stated aim of being a unifying force in British politics.

What next?

Listen to:

- *Guardian* podcast: 'Is the UK ready for Rishi Sunak?' (www.theguardian. com).
- Uncovered podcast: 'What will the Rishi Sunak era look like? A closer look at the new prime minister' (www.nationalworld.com).

Chapter 10

The Supreme Court: the impact of legislative reform and Lord Reed's presidency

Focus

Examination specifications require students to understand the functions of the Supreme Court and its significance within the political system. An emphasis is placed on analysing the court's impact on the executive and legislative branches of government. Students also need to be able to evaluate the significance of decisions made by the Supreme Court, especially those made as part of the judicial review process.

Edexcel	UK Government 4.1	The Supreme Court and its interactions with, and influence over, the legislative and policy making process
AQA	3.1.1.4	The role of the Supreme Court and its impact on government, legislature and policy process

Context

Three developments in the 2000s strengthened the power of the judiciary in the UK. These were the creation of the Supreme Court, the passing of the Human Rights Act and an increase in the use of judicial review. These developments led to an increasing unease within the Conservative government about 'judicial activism'. Conservative politicians felt that judges were using their powers to achieve the social or political outcomes they felt desirable, rather than maintaining political neutrality.

Judges resented the accusations of political activism because they suggested that the judiciary was not fulfilling its professional duties. Judges' and politicians' suspicions of one another persist. In June 2022 the All Party Parliamentary Group on Democracy and the Constitution documented the Conservative government's problematic relationship with the senior judiciary in its report 'An independent judiciary – challenges since 2016'.

2022 saw the Conservative government seeking to deal with judicial activism through legislative change, and the impact of the Judicial Review and Courts Act will be considered below. Fears of judges overstepping the mark have been somewhat calmed in 2022 by an emerging feeling that under Lord Reed's presidency the Supreme Court has been more willing to uphold executive power.

What is judicial review?

Judicial review allows members of the public to challenge the decisions made or actions taken by public bodies. The courts can rule on whether or not public bodies, such as government departments, the devolved assemblies and local authorities, have acted lawfully. Judicial review enables public bodies to be held to account by those they serve. Judges can decide that a public body has exceeded the powers assigned to it or made decisions that have led to unfair outcomes. The powers of judicial review allow judges to strike down decisions they consider to be *ultra vires* – beyond the accepted powers of the public authority. The sovereignty of parliament means the judges have no power to alter or overturn primary legislation (Acts of Parliament).

The Judicial Review and Courts Act 2022

The stated aim of the Judicial Review and Courts Act was to create a more even balance between the powers of government, parliament and the law courts. The act made two key changes to the rules surrounding judicial review. The first change was to the way in which quashing orders can be used by judges.

Box 10.1 | **What are 'quashing orders' and how have they been used until now?**

Quashing orders are what allow judges to strike down secondary legislation (changes to laws made by government ministers, rather than by parliament). They are also the legal tool judges use to cancel any unlawful decisions made by public bodies. Before the passing of the Judicial Review and Courts Act, quashing orders were a blunt instrument. Issuing a quashing order meant declaring that the decision or action being quashed had never had any legal force.

The passing of the Judicial Review and Courts Act gives judges more choice about how they apply quashing orders. For example, quashing orders no longer have to have immediate effect. The act gives judges the ability to suspend a quashing order by announcing that it will be introduced at some point in the future. These so-called suspended quashing orders give a public authority time to make changes to the way it operates. This puts the public authority in control of its response to a ruling that it has acted unlawfully. At the same time, it allows judges to show that they trust the public authority to take the right action to ensure that its future conduct is lawful.

Another difference in the way in which quashing orders can now be used allows judges to require public bodies to change how they operate in future but without declaring any of their past actions illegal. The Johnson government hoped that this new power would prevent situations such as that which followed the judicial review ruling of 2013 that fining benefit claimants for refusing to do unpaid work was unlawful. As a result of this ruling, the government changed the law to make the past fines legal. Today, judges would be able to rule that fines already imposed were lawful but that no further fines should be handed out.

Cart judicial reviews

The second main change brought about by the Judicial Review and Courts Act was the removal of what were known at 'Cart judicial reviews'. These allowed for a re-examination of decisions made by Upper Tribunals, courts which deal with disputes over employment practices, asylum cases, visa applications and requests from those wanting to come to or stay in the UK. Now decisions made by Upper Tribunals will be considered permanent. This means that no other court will have the power to review them. This change to the law was made primarily to reduce the amount of court time spent processing asylum and immigration cases.

The Judicial Review and Courts Act was passed in June 2022 and its impact is not yet apparent. It will almost certainly result in a further fall in judicial review cases, which have been declining steadily since reforms enacted by the Cameron government in 2015. In the first quarter of 2022 there were 550 judicial review cases, 9% down on the first quarter of 2021 and 40% fewer than in the first quarter of 2019. Any further fall in judicial review cases will almost certainly be a result of the abolition of Cart judicial reviews.

The legal profession is unhappy about the ending of Cart judicial reviews. The Law Society has suggested that a legal challenge may be mounted against the change, on the grounds that it could deny people access to justice. The 2022 Supreme Court case Basfar v Wong provides a useful example here. Josephine Wong is a Filipina national who was trafficked to the UK and forced to work in the household of Saudi Arabian diplomat Khalid Basfar. Wong's initial claim against Basfar was rejected by an employment tribunal but she was allowed to appeal her case to the Supreme Court. The latter found in her favour, ruling that Mr Basfar had denied her both fair wages and employment rights. The end of Cart judicial reviews means that Ms Wong's case would not now reach the Supreme Court, denying her the justice our most senior judges felt she deserved.

In its original form, the Judicial Review and Courts bill proposed that judges would only be able to use suspended quashing orders. This proposal drew opposition from the Law Society, the House of Lords, opposition parties in the House of Commons and some Conservative backbenchers, including former home secretary David Davis. A concerted campaign was mounted against the proposal. Those objecting to the change pointed out that it would have restricted the ability of judges to choose how to use quashing orders. The government eventually bowed to the pressure, with the result that judges now have more options than before about how to implement quashing orders. The Law Society declared this to be a major victory for the rule of law in the UK.

Box 10.2 'An independent judiciary — challenges since 2016': a report from the All Party Parliamentary Group on Democracy and the Constitution

In June 2022, the All Party Parliamentary Group on Democracy and the Constitution (APPGDC) published its report into the difficulties facing judges in the UK. The report examines the attitudes of the executive to judges, and the impact of this on the judiciary. The key findings of the report are that judicial decisions are free from political bias and thus that government criticism of judicial decisions is unfair. The report is an important example of the way in which parliament scrutinises the executive.

The APPGDC received written and verbal evidence from a range of legal experts and practising barristers. This evidence informed its report. The Ministry of Justice was invited to give evidence for the report but did not respond to the invitation. Judges were not asked to give evidence in case this opened them up to accusations of improper involvement in politics.

The report is strongly worded from the start. It accuses the executive of undermining public confidence in both the independence of the judiciary and the rule of law in the UK. An example it gives is of the reaction to the trial of those involved in pulling down the statue of slave trader Edward Colston. At the trial, which took place in January 2022 at Bristol Crown Court, the defendants were acquitted of criminal damage by the jury. Rather than showing complete respect for the decision made by the jury, the then attorney general, Suella Braverman, threatened to use her powers to refer the case to the Court of Appeal. She claimed that the acquittal of the defendants had caused 'confusion'. The choice of words left little doubt that she felt the original verdict was the wrong one.

Among the conclusions made in the report is that there is no evidence to support claims made by the executive that the judiciary is becoming more politicised. The report's authors point out that recent 'independent reviews' — the Independent Review of Administrative Law and the Independent Review of the Human Rights Act — were clear that there is no convincing evidence of judges letting political considerations influence their decisions.

The report stops short of asking politicians to cease criticising judges, recognising that politicians, like anyone else, are entitled to free speech. It does though suggest that such attacks are unwise and unhelpful because they undermine the constitutional principle that the judiciary is independent. The attacks also, the report suggests, put pressure on the judiciary to make decisions favourable to the government, so as to avoid further criticism. According to the report, this may explain why since January 2020 the Supreme Court has reversed seven of its previous judgements, a number unprecedented in the history of the court.

The report recommends that the government does more to safeguard the independence of the judiciary. It proposes, for example, that ministers be provided with published guidance 'on their constitutional duties towards the judiciary'. It also advises that greater consideration be given to the appointment of law ministers, such as the lord chancellor and the attorney general. This would involve the prime minister being required to consider whether candidates have the legal qualifications, expertise and experience for the roles to which they are to be appointed. Recommended too is that law ministers be directed to remember that aspects of their job will require them to be apolitical. The report is an important part of the debate about the ongoing role of the executive and the judiciary, but the APPGDC has no power to compel the government into any particular course of action and the government has made no official response to the report.

The Supreme Court under Lord Reed: an end to judicial activism?

Lord Reed, who became President of the Supreme Court in January 2020, seems to have made a conscious decision to rebuild trust between the judiciary and the executive. During meetings with MPs, he has emphasised his understanding of the role of the Supreme Court. Lord Reed thinks that, from a constitutional point of view, disputes between judges and the government are undesirable. He also believes that judges should seek to uphold the separation of powers between the executive and the judiciary. What this means in practice is that judges should not stand in the way of the executive's right to make policy through acts of parliament. In July 2021, Lord Reed dismissed a claim that only allowing parents to receive child benefit for their first two children was a restriction of their right to privacy and family life. Since the policy had been agreed by parliament, Lord Reed wrote in his judgement, the Supreme Court had no right to overturn it.

The number of successful human rights cases was decreasing even before Lord Reed became President of the Supreme Court but has fallen further under his leadership. Today, claimants win fewer than 20% of human rights cases, down from a high of nearly 60% in 2019. At the same time, the number of court cases won by public bodies has increased considerably. Before 2020, fewer than 60% of cases went in favour of the public body, now over 75% do so.

Lord Reed's court: upholding executive power?

The case of R (on the application of O) v Secretary of State for the Home Department concerned whether or not it was lawful for the government to charge an application fee of £1,012 for a child to be registered as a British citizen. The Supreme Court dismissed the argument that the home secretary did not have the right to charge a fee so large that it would effectively prevent some children from being able to become British citizens. As Lord Hodge explained in his judgement of February 2022, parliament had granted the home secretary the power to set the application fee and this meant it was lawful.

In April 2022 the Supreme Court issued its judgement in the case of R (on the application of Coughlan) v Minister for the Cabinet Office. This case concerned the lawfulness of pilot schemes requiring voters to show ID before being allowed to cast their ballots. Lawyers acting for Mr Coughlan, who brought the case, argued that the government was acting *ultra vires* (beyond its powers) in running these pilot schemes. The Supreme Court justices unanimously dismissed the case on the grounds that the pilot schemes were allowed under the terms of the Representation of the People Act, 2000.

Although the cases described above are useful examples of the Supreme Court finding in favour of the executive, they are not evidence of a court that is weak in the face of executive power. The Supreme Court makes fewer rulings against the government but such rulings are made. The case of Secretary of State for the Home Department v SC concerned a Jamaican national, SC, who had been convicted of a violent assault. The court ruled that the home secretary could not order SC's deportation to Jamaica because he might fall victim there to inhuman or degrading treatment. To deport SC would, the court decided, violate his human rights.

There is a difficulty in judging how far Lord Reed's presidency has changed the Supreme Court. His court has not been required to pass judgement on cases as controversial as those that arose during Lady Hale's presidency. The Miller I case, in which the Supreme Court ruled that parliament, not the executive, had the right to trigger Article 50 and begin the process of Britain's departure from the EU, required the court to settle a major constitutional dispute. The Supreme Court would have attracted as much criticism for 'playing politics' if it had ruled in favour of the executive, as it did for ruling against it. Lord Reed does not want his court to be political but it is circumstances, as much as current judicial interpretations of the law, that have contributed to a sense that we are no longer living in an era of judicial activism.

Case Study: The Supreme Court ruling on the Scottish Referendum Bill

In June 2022, the Scottish government published their Scottish Independence Referendum Bill. This set out the details for a second referendum on Scottish Independence. It proposed an advisory vote on the question 'Should Scotland by an independent country?' and suggested a date of 19 October 2023 for the referendum.

The Conservative government objected to the bill on the grounds that matters concerning the relationship between Scotland and the rest of the UK are not devolved to the Scottish parliament but reserved to Westminster. The Scottish government argued that since the referendum was advisory, not binding, it did not infringe on the powers of the UK parliament. The Supreme Court was asked to resolve the matter.

The Supreme Court's ruling issued in November 2022 was that the Scottish Parliament could not hold the referendum. The court's view was that even if the referendum was advisory and had 'no immediate legal consequences', it would still be a 'political event' with 'political consequences'. Lord Reed, summing up the view of the court, explained that in issuing the bill the Scottish Parliament was, therefore, exceeding its power. Only the UK parliament could decide to hold such a referendum. The ruling was welcomed by Rishi Sunak as 'clear and definitive'. The Conservative Party remains committed to preserving the union of England and Scotland. Scotland's first minister, Nicola Sturgeon, said she respected the court's decision but that she was disappointed because 'the ruling blocks one route to Scotland's voice being heard on independence.'

Exam success

The amount of power the Supreme Court exercises within the UK political system continues to be an important area of discussion. Questions in this area may be framed as follows:

- *Evaluate how far the Supreme Court is willing and able to check executive power.* (Edexcel style, 30 marks)
- *'The Supreme Court is willing and able to check executive power.' Analyse and evaluate this statement.* (AQA style, 25 marks)

The best responses to these questions will consider the context within which the Supreme Court operates by examining the powers it has within the British constitution. This will allow for an assessment of how far the Supreme Court is able to check executive power. They will also analyse recent Supreme Court data and judgements to evaluate how far the Supreme Court seems willing to challenge executive power. The best essays will focus on the following themes:

- The limited powers of the Supreme Court. One example of its limited powers is that it can strike down secondary but not primary legislation. Another is that although the Human Rights Act allows the Supreme Court to declare that other laws are incompatible with human rights, such a declaration does not compel the government to change the law.
- The fact that the Supreme Court cannot decide for itself what matters to investigate. It can only rule on issues brought before it. Crucially, though, these issues may be ones of constitutional importance, which allow the Supreme Court to rule on what powers the executive is entitled to exercise. The Miller I and Miller II cases are useful examples of this.
- The extent to which judicial review is an effective check on executive power. Relevant here will be examples of the Supreme Court ruling that the executive has acted *ultra vires*, as well as examples of the Supreme Court upholding executive power.

What next?

Read: 'An independent judiciary — challenges since 2016: an inquiry into the impact of the actions and rhetoric of the Executive since 2016 on the constitutional role of the Judiciary', a report by the All Party Parliamentary Group on Democracy and the Constitution (www.jonathandjanogly.com).